Test Your Phrasal Verbs

Jake Allsop

D1343293

PENGUIN ENGLISH

Pearson Education Limited
Edinburgh Gate
Harlow
Essex CM20 2JE, England
and Associated Companies throughout the world.

ISBN-13: 978-0-582-45171-1
ISBN-10: 0-582-45171-X

First published 1990
This edition published 2002

Sixth impression, 2006

Text copyright © Jake Allsop 1990, 2002

Designed and typeset by Pantek Arts Ltd, Maidstone, Kent
Test Your format devised by Peter Watcyn-Jones
Illustrations by Phil Healey, Gillian Martin and Ross Thomson
Printed in China
SWTC/06

Acknowledgements
The author would like to thank the editors at Penguin, led by Helen Parker
and Jane Durkin, for their skilful, supportive and sensitive editing.

Published by Pearson Education Limited in association with Penguin Books Ltd, both
companies being subsidiaries of Pearson plc.

For a complete list of the titles available from Penguin English please visit our
website at www.penguinenglish.com, or write to your local Pearson Education office
or to: Penguin English Marketing Department, Pearson Education, Edinburgh Gate,
Harlow, Essex CM20 2JE.

Contents

To the student

Phrasal verbs are compound verbs consisting of a verb, like *come* or *take*, and a particle (i.e. an adverb or a preposition), like *off* or *up*. They are a common and important part of English, especially in speaking and in informal writing. Often they have an equivalent formal word, for example, *make up* (informal phrasal verb), and *invent* (formal equivalent). New phrasal verbs are being created all the time, particularly by young people.

Phrasal verbs ('phrasals') are not difficult to learn and use, but you cannot always guess the meaning of a phrasal from its verb and particle. In addition, you need to be aware that the same phrasal verb can have more than one meaning. The verb *take off*, for example, has several different meanings: you can **take off** (*remove*) your coat, you can **take off** (*imitate*) a person, and an aeroplane can **take off** (*leave the ground*). This book will help you test and increase your knowledge of phrasal verbs, starting with combinations of the most common verbs and particles.

There are 9 sections in this book. They will help you to use and understand:

- phrasal verbs with more than one meaning;
- formal and informal equivalents;
- idioms using phrasal verbs;
- three-part phrasal verbs (when a phrasal verb is followed by a preposition, e.g. *put up with*);
- adjectives and nouns formed from phrasal verbs, e.g. **pick-up** truck (adjective) and **outcome** (noun).

Each section begins with a short explanation of the points being tested, and most tests also have tips (advice) on how to do the test and what to look out for. Do read these explanations and tips: they are there to help you. There is also an Answers section at the back of the book so that you can check your answers.

There is no magic formula for learning phrasal verbs, but you should always consider the various meanings of the particle as well as the meaning of the verb. For example, the particle *down* has different meanings in the following phrases: *cut* **down** *a tree*, *turn* **down** *an offer* and *write* **down** *your address*.

When you come across a phrasal verb which is new to you, it is a good idea to learn it in a context. So, for example, don't simply learn '*make up* means *invent*'; learn '**make up** *a story*' or '*It isn't true: I just **made** it **up***'.

Look out not just for phrasal verbs, but also for adjectives and nouns formed from them: they are a rich part of the English language. Above all, phrasal verbs are fun. Enjoy them.

Jake Allsop

Section 1: Common verbs used in phrasal verbs

A phrasal verb consists of a VERB like *come*, *get*, *give* combined with a PARTICLE like *up*, *on*, *away*, to give phrasal verbs like *come up*, *get on*, *give away*.

Sometimes the phrasal verb has a literal (everyday) meaning, e.g. *to come up the hill*, *to get on a bus*, *to give all your money away*.

More often, the phrasal verb has a non-literal (transferred) meaning, e.g. *to come up to someone* (approach them), *to get on well* (to make progress), *to give away a secret* (to tell it to someone else).

The verbs used in phrasal verbs are usually very common like *come*, *go*, *get*, *take* – as in this section – but sometimes phrasal verbs are made from more uncommon verbs, e.g. *pop in* (visit someone without warning), *crop up* (arise), *butt in* (interrupt).

'We had a strange bird in the garden the other day.'
'What was it like?'

1 Phrasal verbs with *be, come, get, go* or *take*

Complete these sentences by adding the correct verb from the box. In some cases, you will need to change the tense or form of the verb.

> be about   be for   ~~be like~~   come back   come from
> come off   get back   get in   get up   go away
> go on   go with   take back   take down   take off

1 'There was a strange bird in the garden the other day.'
'What _was_ it _like_ ?'
'It was grey with long legs and a long beak.'

2 'Do you like my new green-and-purple T-shirt?'
'Well, it's very nice, but it doesn't really _____ _____ your pink-and-orange trousers.'

3 I lost the keys to my apartment, so I had to _____ _____ through a window.

4 I bought a mobile phone, but it didn't work, so I _____ it _____ to the shop and they gave me another one.

5 I asked my father where babies _____ _____, and he said 'the Maternity Hospital'.

6 'Leave my house at once, and never _____ _____!'

7 As I was walking down the stair*, I met a man who wasn't there. He wasn't there again today: Oh, how I wish he'd _____ _____!

---

* *Stair* (singular) meaning a flight of steps is poetic; in modern English we always refer to *stairs* (plural).

8   'Right now, I am reading a book called *Fermat's Last Theorem.'*
'How interesting. What _____ it _____?'
'I have no idea!'

9   If I invest in the Flat Earth Company, I'll be lucky to _____ my money _____, let alone make a profit.

10   We put up a poster to advertise our concert, but so many people complained about it that we had to _____ it _____.

11   There is a key on computer keyboards labelled 'Alt Gr', but nobody knows what it _____ _____!

12   They say a plane _____ _____ from O'Hare Airport in Chicago every four seconds. It must be a very busy airport!

13   'I'd really like to ask Michael for a date, but I am afraid he will say no.'
'_____ _____, ask him. I know for a fact that he really likes you!'

14   I hit a stone while I was cycling, the wheel _____ _____ and I went head over heels into the hedge!

15   I like to sleep late on Sundays because I have to _____ _____ so early during the week.

Come suggests *from another place to here.*
Go suggests *from here to another place.*
Get literally means either *obtain* or *become.*
Take literally means *carry from here to another place.*
Be is a joining verb as in *she is an engineer.*

2 Phrasal verbs with *be*

SECTION 1

Complete these sentences by adding the correct particle from the box.

about	after	around	~~away~~	back	for	from	into
	like	off	on	over	through	up	with

1. 'Is your boss in?'
   'No, I'm afraid she's __away__ on leave at the moment.'

2. 'When will she be _____?'
   'Not until next Wednesday.'

3. 'What a complicated instrument panel! What's this red button _____?'
   'It's the ejector seat. Please don't pre...'

4. 'Shall we watch some television?'
   'If you like. What's _____?'

5. 'Where are you _____?'
   'Birmingham.'

6. 'What is Birmingham _____?'
   'I don't know. I left there when I was three months old, and I've never been back since.'

7. 'I'm reading a novel called *Moby Dick*.'
   'What's it _____?'
   'Whales.'
   '*Moby Dick* doesn't sound like a Welsh name to me!'

8. The traffic was so bad that by the time we got to the theatre, the concert was almost _____.

9 'Haven't you finished yet?'
'Don't worry, I'm nearly _____.'

10 'Please hurry up!'
'OK, I'll be _____ you in just a second.'

11 'What's _____? You look as if you had seen a ghost!'
'Who said that?'

12 It's getting late. I'd better be _____ before my father sends
out a search party.

13 [people chatting to each other online:]

'I'm busy chatting to someone at the moment, but I'd love to
have a chat with you too. Will you be _____ for a while yet?'
'I won't log off for at least half an hour, I promise.'

14 Rob is forever changing hobbies. Last year it was bird-watching.
Now, he's really _____ stamp collecting.

15 'That's the third time this week that my sister has phoned me. I
wonder what she's _____.'
'Maybe she isn't _____ anything. Maybe she just wants to
talk to you.'

Be literally tells us that something exists, as in *There is food in the
refrigerator.*
Be is often a joining verb, as in *She is an engineer.*

3 Phrasal verbs with *come*

Complete these sentences by adding the correct particle from the box.

about	across	along	~~back~~	before	forward	from
in	into	off	on	out	round	to	up

1   A boomerang is a hunting weapon. It is shaped so that it will come __*back*__ to the person who throws it.

2   'Where do you come _____?'
    'Thailand.'

3   Please come _____! Make yourself at home.

4   F comes _____ G in the alphabet.

5   Why don't you come _____ to our house for dinner on Saturday?

6   The sergeant asked for volunteers, but only three came _____.

7   Just look at these old photographs. I came _____ them when I was clearing out an old cupboard.

8   'What magazine is that?'
    'It's a literary magazine called *The Bookworm*.'
    'How often does it come _____?'
    'Monthly.'

9   Oh dear! Pollution, global warming, the hole in the ozone layer: I don't know what the world is coming _____!

10 'Come _____, Philip. Everyone else has finished except you!'

11   We're all going out for a pizza. Would you like to come _____?

12   I hear that Michelle has come _____ a lot of money. Her rich aunt died and left her half a million.

13   Every time the subject of holidays comes _____, Ruth and her husband have an argument.

14   Pauline is working on a plan to convert her farmhouse into a bed and breakfast place. She reckons she'll make a fortune if it comes _____.

15   There has been another big crash on the freeway just south of LA. How did it come _____?

A boomerang is shaped so that it will come back to the person who throws it.

Come, in sentences 1, 3, 5 and 6, refers literally to a movement *from another place to here.*

Section 1: Common verbs used in phrasal

4 Phrasal verbs with *get*

In this story some of the particles are wrong. Write the correct particles in the column on the right. Choose from the words in the box.

~~across~~ away back behind down into on over round to

The river was flooded and Carole and I weren't
sure how we would be able to get *into*.

1   *across*

'Let's take that boat we saw upstream,'
I suggested.

'No way!' Carole replied. 'That's stealing,
and anyway, we'd never get *behind* with it!'

2   _____

We decided to make a raft out of some logs.
Carole tore her shirt into strips to tie them
together, and then the two of us got *round*
to the raft.

3   _____

Just at that moment, a huge log came
floating downstream and Carole shouted
to me to get *to*.

4   _____

We managed to leap back on to the bank
just as the log hit our raft and smashed
it to pieces.

'We'll never get *down* the other side now!'
I said in despair.

5   _____

ᵓn't worry, every problem has a solution.
ʰink of something. We'll get *across*
ᵛ,' Carole said cheerfully. She went
ᵓdge and stepped in. It wasn't
current was really swift.

6   _____

ᵒn verbs used in phrasal verbs

'Come on, silly!' she said, 'I <u>got you **on**</u>   7   _____
this mess and I'll get you out of it!'

She turned and smiled at me.

'<u>Get **over**</u> me and hold me round the waist,'   8   _____
she said, 'until I can find out how deep it is.'

With the water up to her knees, she signalled
to me to climb on her shoulders. She went
slowly, pausing with each step to make sure
she had a firm foothold. Suddenly, I felt her
slip. I screamed, but fortunately she regained
her balance. When we were in shallow water,
she told me it was safe for me to <u>get **away**</u>.   9   _____

I think we both realised how close we had
come to drowning in the swirling waters, and
it took us a long time to <u>get **back**</u> the experience.   10   _____

Get literally describes a change from one state to another, as in *get angry*
i.e. *become angry*.
Get sometimes means *receive* or *obtain*, as in *get a rise in salary*.

Section 1: Common verbs used in phrase

5 Phrasal verbs with *go*

A phrasal verb is wrong in each of the following sentences. Write the correct words.

1. One by one, the street lights went on, leaving us in total darkness.

   the street lights went off

2. The letter was returned to the sender with the words 'Gone over, no longer at this address' written on it.

   _____

3. 'I thought you liked Country and Western music.'
   'Well, I used to, but I've really gone for it lately.'

   _____

4. There's an awful flu virus going up. I hope you don't catch it.

   _____

5. What a fascinating story. Do go away!

   _____

6. Mark was sure that he had picked up his key, but when he went outside his pockets, he couldn't find it anywhere.

   _____

7. I don't think that red blouse really goes for your orange miniskirt, Sophie.

   _____

verbs

.non verbs used in phrasal verbs

8 'Did you know that camels can go under water for thirty days?'
'They must get very thirsty!'

___

9 What a lot of people! Do you think there will be enough food to
go without?

___

10 This is a very complex computer program. You might need to go
by the instructions again before you get the hang of it.

___

'I thought you liked Country and Western music.'
'Well, I used to...'

Go suggests *from here to another place*, i.e. the opposite of *come*.
Go also describes a change from one state to another, as in *Don't let
the fire go out*.

6 Phrasal verbs with *take*

Replace each word in **CAPITALS** with a phrasal verb containing the verb *take*. Choose from the particles in the box. In some cases, you will need to change the tense or form of the verb.

after	back	~~down~~	in	off	on	out	over	up

1. 'Why have you **REMOVED** all the pictures in the sitting- room?'
'Because I'm going to decorate it.'
taken down

2. 'This radio I bought only picks up Radio Ulan Bator.'
'Why don't you **RETURN** it to the shop where you bought it, then?'
_____

3. Is *The Economist* a very good magazine? Because, if it is, I might **START** a subscription.
_____

4. I'm not very fit, so I've decided to **ADOPT** an active hobby such as squash or jogging.
_____

5. The Worldwide Chemicals Company was recently **BOUGHT** by its biggest rival.
_____

6. 'What did you think of Tanga airport?'
'Very nice, but our plane couldn't **LEAVE** until all the goats had been chased off the runway.'
_____

7. 'Does John **RESEMBLE** his mother or his father?'
'Well, he looks just like his father, but he has his mother's ears.'
_____

8 One day, I painted little red spots all over my face, and told my father that I had caught measles. For a moment he was completely **FOOLED**, but then he realised that it was a joke. _____

9 'Dad, is it all right if I leave school and get married?'
'I can't advise you on that. You'd better **DISCUSS** it with your mother.' _____

10 Because nobody else wanted to do it, Ms Van Winkle agreed to **ASSUME** the role of Director of Public Relations in the Ministry of Industry. _____

The airport was very nice but...

 Take literally means *carry from one place to another place.*
Take is used in many idiomatic expressions such as *take up a hobby.*

7 Find the caption 1

Match the correct caption with each cartoon.

a 'OK, I give up. How did you get them across?'

b 'You can see she takes after her father.'

c 'I don't think he is really up to it.'

d 'Do you think this cheese has gone off?'

e 'She comes across as a very bossy person.'

1

_____

2

_____

3

_____

4

_____

5

_____

Section 2: Common particles used in phrasal verbs

The meaning of a phrasal verb is often in the PARTICLE rather than in the VERB.

Sometimes, the particle has its literal (normal) meaning, e.g. *run up* (the stairs), where *up* means *from a lower to a higher place*.

Sometimes, the particle has a slightly transferred (non-literal) meaning, e.g. *turn up* (the volume on the radio), where *up* indicates *an increase of some kind*.

Sometimes, the particle has a completely transferred meaning, e.g. *drink up*, where *up* means *fully and completely*.

In an identity parade a witness is asked to pick out the suspect from the others.

8 Phrasal verbs with *off*

Circle the following statements True or False.

1 CALL OFF
To postpone an event is to call it off.   **True** (**False**)

2 CUT OFF
A town surrounded by floodwater is completely
cut off.   **True**   **False**

3 COME OFF
A plan that fails to work is one that comes off.   **True**   **False**

4 FIGHT OFF
You would be very miserable if you fought
off a cold.   **True**   **False**

5 GET OFF
To leave a bus or a train is to get off.   **True**   **False**

6 GO OFF
You would try to avoid drinking milk that
had gone off.   **True**   **False**

7 PUT OFF
If you postpone a meeting, you put it off.   **True**   **False**

8 RING OFF
To ring off is to change your mind about
getting married.   **True**   **False**

9 TIP OFF
The police use informers who tip them
off if a crime is about to be committed.   **True**   **False**

10 HOLD OFF
If the rain holds off, we can continue
playing tennis.   **True**   **False**

What does *off* mean?
a) move from one place to another, as in *fall off your bike*
b) disconnect, as in *switch off the light*
c) disappear, as in *the effect of a drug wears off*

9 Phrasal verbs with *down*, *in*, *off*, *out* or *away*

Complete these sentences by adding the correct verb from the box. In some cases, you will need to change the tense or form of the verb.

break	call	chop	come	cut	drop	~~get~~	go
lie	put	see	stay	take	take	throw	

1. Never ___get___ off a bus while it is still moving!

2. 'Waiter, there's a fly in my soup. Please _____ it away.'
   'I am sorry, sir, but I don't know how to catch flies!'

3. 'Do you know where my newspaper is, dear?'
   'Oh, I thought you had finished with it, so I _____ it away. Sorry!'

4. I picked up the book, but when I found that it was about Quantum Mechanics, I quickly _____ it down again.

5. The tree next to my house had become so dangerous that I had to _____ it down.

6. 'Where's grandma?'
   'She said she felt tired, so she's gone to _____ down on her bed.'

7. In March, it's often warm enough to sit in the garden when the sun is out, but once the sun _____ in, everybody rushes back into the house!

8. We haven't seen you for ages! Why don't you _____ in for a cup of coffee the next time you are passing the house?

9. When we got back from our holiday, we found that thieves had _____ in and stolen all our furniture.

10 Both my children caught bad colds and had to _____ away from school for a week.

11 My sister was at the airport to _____ me off, and she was there to meet me when I got back.

12 'How do you get into the watch to repair it?'
'Easy! Look, the back _____ off.'

13 Will you please _____ the dog out for a walk? I'd do it myself, but I haven't got time.

14 Rachel loves animals, so whenever she sees pictures of animals in a magazine, she _____ them out and puts them up on the wall of her bedroom.

15 When I opened the book, a piece of paper _____ out. When I picked it up, I realised it was a secret message.

Never get off a bus while it is still moving!

10 Phrasal verbs with *in*

Complete these sentences by adding the correct verb from the box. In some cases, you will need to change the tense or form of the verb.

break	bring	buy	call	deal	dig	draw	get
give	go	hand	keep	show	stay	trade	

1 How on earth did the robbers manage to ___*break*___ in without anyone seeing them?

2 'Are you going out tonight?'
'No, I've got to _____ in and wash my hair.'

3 He twisted my arm to make me tell what I knew, but I refused to _____ in.

4 If you feel like crying, cry. Express your feelings: don't _____ them in.

5 'It's Ms Smith to see you, sir.'
'_____ her in!'

6 You _____ the food in and I'll buy the drinks, and we'll have a bit of a party.

7 'Has Fred been round to see you lately?'
'Well, as a matter of fact, he said that he would be _____ in today on his way home from work.'

8 'Have you done your essay?'
'Of course! I _____ it in last week.'

9 I've decided to _____ in my old car for a new one.

10 We _____ in enough food to last us through the winter.

11 The days are really _____ in now: it's already dark by five o'clock at this time of year.

12 It's quite cold now that the sun's _____ in. Do you really want to go for a swim in the river now?

13 Help yourself! _____ in! There's enough food and drink for everybody!

14 Nowadays, most multinationals _____ in more than one range of products. For example, an oil company might also _____ in cosmetics, plastics and food.

15 I see this crazy government has just _____ in a new law making it illegal for shops to sell water pistols to children under sixteen.

What does *in* mean?
a) be inside a place or move into a place as in *stay in* (not go out);
b) out of sight, as in *the sun has gone in.*

11 Phrasal verbs with *down*

Column A contains definitions of phrasal verbs with DOWN. Column B contains simple phrases or sentences in which you might use the phrasal verb. Complete each phrase in Column B using a phrasal verb with DOWN.

	Column A Definition	Column B Example of use
1	dismount	It's not easy to g*et down* off a camel.
2	remove	t_____ the curtains in order to wash them
3	refuse	t_____ an offer, such as a marriage proposal
4	stop functioning	Machines b_____ when they are neglected.
5	reduce	c_____ on the amount of coffee you drink
6	fall (of prices)	Prices only c_____ during sales.
7	despise	Don't l_____ on people just because they are poor.
8	let go of	too exciting a book to p_____
9	rest	If you're tired, go and l_____ .
10	suppress	Governments always try to p_____ demonstrations and riots.

11 make a note of   Did you w_____ my details in your
                        address book?

12 locate   t_____ a phone number in the phone
                        book

13 erode   In time, water will always w_____ the
                        hardest rock.

14 resign   s_____ as President and go into
                        retirement

15 disappoint   l_____ someone by failing to keep
                        your promise

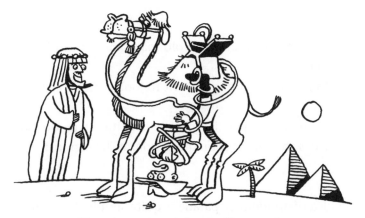

It's not easy to get down off a camel.

What does *down* mean?

a) from a higher to a lower place, as in *run down the hill*

b) destroy, as in *cut down a tree*

c) no longer in working order, as in *break down*

d) refuse, deny, as in *turn down an application*

e) record something, as in *write down an answer*

12 Phrasal verbs with *out*

Complete these sentences by inserting the correct verb from the box. In some cases, you will need to change the tense or form of the verb.

cut	drop	~~dry~~	fall	help	pass	pick	rub
show	slip	stand	take	throw	wipe	work	

1 Charlie hung his wet socks on the clothesline and they soon ___*dried*___ out in the hot sun.

2 To celebrate my examination success, my parents _____ me out for dinner.

3 Pauline is a great Manchester United fan. She _____ out all the newspaper articles about the team and pastes them in a scrapbook.

4 'Do you really want all these old magazines or can I _____ them out?'
'No, don't do that. I might want to look at them again one day.'

5 Don always uses a pencil when he is writing a report, so that, if he decides to remove something from it, he can just _____ it out.

6 The idea of an identity parade is quite simple. You stand a number of people in a line, including the suspected person. Then a witness is asked to _____ out the suspect from the others.

7 It looks as if Sophie and her husband have _____ out again: they're not speaking to each other.

8   Mr Kafka could never have found his way out of the building by himself, so it was a good thing that the boss's secretary offered to _____ him out.

9   'I hear that you and Vivienne have split up. What happened?'
'Well, we tried to make a go of it, but things just didn't _____ out as we had hoped.'

10   Justine is doing voluntary work in her spare time: she is _____ out at the old people's home in Winton.

11   After the first year, very few students _____ out: most go on to complete their studies.

12   'Where's Jonathan?'
'He won't be long. He's just _____ out to Video Rentals to get a couple of videos.'

13   'Do you like my new pink suit with the large blue spots on it?'
'Well, it certainly makes you _____ out from the crowd.'

14   If I could win the lottery, I could _____ out all my debts in one go.

15   Some people are so nervous they _____ out at the sight of blood.

What does *out* mean?
a) be outside a place or move out of a place, as in *run out of the room*;
b) (cause to) fade or completely disappear, as in *put the light out*;
c) become or be clearer or louder, as in *work out an answer*;
d) distribute or give to each one, as in *hand out leaflets*.

13 Phrasal verbs with *away*

Choose the word which best fits in these sentences.

1 Several children had to ___stay___ away from school because of the bus strike.

a) play b) stay c) go

2 Did you ever play that silly game of knocking on someone's door and then _____ away?

a) banging b) turning c) running

3 'I'd like a pizza marinara, please.'
'To eat here or to _____ away?'

a) take b) put c) throw

4 If you don't like injections, it's a good idea to _____ away when the doctor sticks the needle in.

a) pass b) turn c) look

5 We decided to _____ away from the main party and form a new party called the Lunatic Party.

a) stand b) break c) slide

6 He says the house is haunted, but I think that it's a story designed to _____ children away.

a) beat b) explain c) frighten

7 I didn't want to disturb anyone, so I just _____ away quietly without saying goodbye.

a) slipped b) shot c) ripped

8 If you park illegally in London, the police will either clamp your car or _____ it away.

    a) blow   b) tow   c) row

9 'Old soldiers never die, They simply _____ away' (song)

    a) fade   b) fire   c) fall

10 The old tramp asked for something to eat, but the farmer _____ him away empty-handed.

    a) pushed   b) took   c) sent

What does *away* mean?

a) from here to another place, as in *go away*, *throw away*

b) slowly getting less or weakening, disappearing, as in *die away* (of a sound)

c) continuously or without stopping, as in *work away* (at a task)

14 Find the caption 2

Add the missing particles to the captions and then match the correct caption to each cartoon.

| a | 'You should have seen the fish that got _____!' |

| b | 'He has slowed _____ a lot since his operation.' |

| c | 'How nice of you to drop _____!' |

| d | 'Attendance has been dropping _____ lately.' |

| e | 'I'll soon work it _____.' |

1   _____

2   _____

3

4

5

Section 3: Phrasal verbs with more than one meaning

A phrasal verb may have several meanings. It may have a literal meaning, e.g. *when one car **bumps into** another car* (one car hits another). Or it may have a slightly transferred non-literal meaning, e.g. *when you **bump into** an old friend* (meet a friend by chance).

But often the meaning can only be guessed from the context, e.g. *I wanted to buy a new computer, but I was **put off** by the price* (it cost more than I wanted to pay).

'It's really cold tonight, please don't let the fire go out.'

15 Match the objects

Match the sentences in Group A with the pairs of objects listed in Group B.

Group A

1	Two things that you can blow up	_g_
2	Two things that you can break off	_____
3	Two things that you can bump into	_____
4	Two things that you can cover up	_____
5	Two things that you can give away	_____
6	Two things that you can look up	_____
7	Two things that you can make up	_____
8	Two things that you run across	_____
9	Two things that you can see through	_____
10	Two things that you can take back	_____

Group B

a   a stain on the carpet and facts that you don't want other people to know

b   your face and a story

c   a tree in the dark and a friend you haven't seen for a while

d   what someone owes you and something unkind that you said

e   all your money and a secret

f   a field and something you didn't expect to find

g   a balloon and a photograph

h   a piece of bread and an engagement to be married

i   a chimney and a word in the dictionary

j   a lace curtain and a crazy scheme

16 Two meanings 1

Each sentence in Group 1 uses the same phrasal verb as a sentence in Group 2, but with a change of meaning. Insert the following verbs into the sentences and then find the pairs and complete the table below. You may need to change the form of the verb.

cut down	fall out	fall through	go off	go out
hang up	look into	make up	~~put off~~	stand for

Group 1

1. I like the taste of Gorgonzola cheese, but the smell __*puts*__ me __*off*__ .

2. Put the milk in the refrigerator or it will _____ _____ .

3. Richard is a typical untidy boy: he never _____ his clothes _____ .

4. Jill opened her purse, turned it upside down and all her money _____ _____.

5. There used to be a lovely wood here, but the farmer _____ all the trees _____ .

6. What do the letters *Ctrl* _____ _____ on a computer keyboard?

7. My little brother _____ _____ a hole in the ice and nearly drowned.

8. Is it true that your mother is an astronaut, or did you just _____ that _____?

9. _____ _____ my eyes and tell me what you see there!

10. I never _____ _____ after dark; I prefer to stay in and surf the internet.

Group 2

a The film *Titanic* has encouraged several groups to _____ _____ ways of raising the sunken ship.

b If someone phones you trying to sell you something, don't waste your time: just _____ _____!

c 'I thought you were going to move to a new house.'

'We were, but the buyers of our old house changed their minds, and the sale _____ _____.'

d There'll be a riot if they ban the wearing of baseball caps back to front: students won't _____ _____ it.

e The group's drummer is ill, so they have had to __*put*__ __*off*__ their rehearsal until next Friday.

f 'Don't let the sun set on your anger,' they say. So let's kiss and _____ _____!

g I used to like horror movies, but I've _____ _____ them lately.

h It's really cold tonight; please don't let the fire _____ _____.

i Jane and Ann are really good friends, but they have _____ _____ and are not speaking to each other.

j If you really want to lose weight, you should _____ _____ on carbohydrates and fatty foods.

1	2	3	4	5	6	7	8	9	10
e									

Think of the meaning of the verb, and think of the meaning of the particle. For example, *cut* and *down* are used literally in *cut down a tree*, but non-literally in *cut down on* (reduce) *the amount of fat you eat.*

17 Two meanings 2

Each sentence in Group 1 uses the same phrasal verb as a sentence in Group 2, but with a change of meaning. Insert the following verbs into the sentences and then find the pairs and complete the table below. You may need to change the form of the verb.

break off	~~cut out~~	drop in	give away	hang up
look into	tear off	turn in	turn round	tuck in

Group 1

1. Whenever there was an article in the sports section of the newspaper about the New York Yankees, Sue would always __cut__ it __out__ and send it to her sister in San Diego.

2. I don't need these old clothes. I think I'll just _____ them _____.

3. Please _____ _____ and see us any time you are in Tucson.

4. It's getting late: I think I'll _____ _____.

5. My children are too lazy to open the milk carton with scissors: they just _____ the top _____.

6. Every time I _____ _____ the mirror, I find more spots on my chin.

7. Japan and China could not agree on an agenda, so they decided to _____ _____ negotiations.

8. Every night, Dad goes upstairs to tell the kids a story, _____ them _____ and kisses them goodnight.

9. The company was losing money last year, but this year we have managed to _____ it _____.

10. (On the telephone) 'Please don't _____ _____ until I have had a chance to tell you how sorry I am.'

Group 2

a The food looked so delicious that we all started to _____
_____ without being asked.

b All the newspapers are full of the story about the 75-year-old
woman who _____ _____ her clothes and dived into the
river to save a child from drowning.

c Don't laugh or you'll _____ the game _____.

d If you are overweight, it is a good idea to reduce the amount of
sugar you eat, and in fact it is better if you can __*cut*__ it
__*out*__ completely.

e Children! Don't throw your coats on the chair. _____ them
_____ properly in the wardrobe.

f If your friend offered you stolen goods, would you _____
_____ him to the authorities?

g 'Liz, there's a problem with the CD drive. It won't open.'
'I'm busy right now, Bob. I'll _____ _____ it later.'

h What a lovely dress! Please _____ _____ so that I can see
what it is like at the back.

i Open the box and _____ your money _____ .

j Please _____ _____ some pieces of chocolate and give them
to the children.

1	2	3	4	5	6	7	8	9	10
d									

18 Two meanings 3

Complete the cartoon captions using the phrasal verbs from the box. Each phrasal verb is used twice but with different meanings. You may need to change the tense or form of the verb.

come off	take off	switch off

1 'The artist has tried to give the idea of "Young Love" but I don't think it quite _comes_ _off_ .'

2 'It's not likely to
_____ _____
today, is it?'

3 'Don't forget to _____ _____ the light before you go to bed.'

4 'Are they supposed to
_____ _____ like
that?'

5 'He never _____ his
hat _____ in public.'

6 'When he is bored, he
simply _____
_____.'

19 Two meanings 4

Each sentence in Group 1 uses the same phrasal verb as a sentence in Group 2, but with a change of meaning. Insert the following verbs into the sentences and then find the pairs and complete the table below. You may need to change the form of the verb.

catch on	dry up	fall off	fall through	look up
make up	put off	run across	see through	take back

Group 1

1 There's a hole in the floor. Mind you don't __*fall*__ __*through*__ it.

2 Whenever there is a period without rain, all the lakes _____ _____.

3 The President is very popular, but not with me: her false smile really _____ me _____.

4 They quarrel every morning, but they always _____ _____ afterwards.

5 I've had some bad luck lately, but things are beginning to _____ _____, I'm glad to say.

6 Once you have started something, you ought to _____ it _____ to the end.

7 Hold the handlebars with both hands or you might _____ _____!

8 This coat I bought is too small for me. Do you think I should _____ it _____ to the shop?

9 Have you seen Ethan lately? Yes, I happened to _____ _____ him in Ankara a couple of months ago.

10 Janet's children are very intelligent. When you explain something to them, they seem to _____ _____ very quickly.

Group 2

a   If you don't know the meaning of a word, you can always
_____ it _____ in the dictionary.

b   Is that a true story, or did you just _____ it _____?

c   Sword swallowing is very popular in Albania, they tell me. Do you
think it will ever _____ _____ here?

d   Actors hate it when they forget their words, and simply _____
_____.

e   It is dangerous to let children _____ _____ busy roads.

f   He tried to deceive her with his talk about marriage, but she was
able to _____ _____ him very easily.

g   We've made all the arrangements. Let's hope our plans don't
___*fall*___ __*through*__ at the last moment.

h   I said that Jim was a lazy good-for-nothing, but I was wrong: I
_____ _____ everything I said about him.

i   We used to get a lot of people at our meetings, but attendance has
started to _____ _____ lately.

j   The launch of the Pluto satellite, which was scheduled for today,
has been _____ _____ until next week for technical reasons.

1	2	3	4	5	6	7	8	9	10
g									

Think of the meaning of the verb, and think of the meaning of the particle.
For example, *see* and *through* may be used literally, as in *see through the
window* or they may be used non-literally as in *see through* (not be fooled
by) *a dishonest scheme.*

20 Two meanings 5

Complete the cartoon captions using the phrasal verbs from the box. Each phrasal verb is used twice but with different meanings. You may need to change the tense or form of the verb.

> go out   put back   blow up

1   He _goes_ _out_ at the same time every night.

2   'Please _____ all the bones _____ in their proper place.'

3   'That's the end of the summer. Time to _____ the clocks _____.'

4 'But WHY do you want to _____ _____ the Houses of Parliament?'

5 'Come on, _____ _____ the balloon and let's get started'

6 'Now, don't let the fire _____ _____!'

21 Two meanings 6

Each sentence in Group 1 uses the same phrasal verb as a sentence in Group 2, but with a change of meaning. Insert the following verbs into the sentences and then find the pairs and complete the table below. You may need to change the form of the verb.

> bump into   clear up   cover up   cut down   leak out
> ~~let off~~   look over   play at   set off   stand by

Group 1

1   He should have gone to prison but the judge ___*let*___ him ___*off*___ with a caution.

2   I _____ _____ what I said: I refuse to take back a word of it.

3   There is a wonderful view from our back window, because we _____ _____ the golf course.

4   It's raining quite heavily at the moment, but I hope it will _____ _____ later in time for the barbecue.

5   There was a lovely old oak tree in the garden, but it became so big that we had to _____ it _____.

6   In many countries, women tourists are advised to wear long dresses with long sleeves in order to _____ _____ their arms and legs.

7   I happened to _____ _____ Kate the other day; I hadn't seen her for ages.

8   The Los Angeles rush hour can be awful, so it's a good idea to _____ _____ early to avoid the traffic.

9   What do you think you're _____ _____? Stop that at once!

10   No matter how hard you try to keep a secret, it always _____ _____ sooner or later.

Group 2

a   The bright colours of the roses were _____ _____ by the soft yellow brick of the garden wall.

b   There was a hole in the bottom of the flask, and all the liquid _____ _____.

c   Although it seemed just the house we wanted, we decided to _____ _____ it very carefully before making up our minds to buy it.

d   It is very dangerous to __*let*__ __*off*__ fireworks when holding them in your hand.

e   'After a party, do you _____ _____ the mess right away, or do you leave it until the next morning?'
    'I leave it, and hope my partner will do it for me!'

f   The children were in the garden _____ _____ cowboys and Indians.

g   A large man _____ _____ me the other day, and practically knocked me over.

h   You really ought to stop smoking, but if you can't, then you should at least try to _____ _____ to no more than three or four a day.

i   A woman is attacked in the street. Instead of going to help her, other people just _____ _____ and watch. Isn't that terrible?

j   It is the instinct of politicians to _____ _____ the truth about their mistakes, and the duty of journalists to expose them.

1	2	3	4	5	6	7	8	9	10
d									

Section 4: Nouns and adjectives formed from phrasal verbs

Nouns and adjectives formed from phrasal verbs may have a literal or a transferred (non-literal) meaning. There are two patterns for these nouns and adjectives formed from phrasal verbs. The first type (literal) is much more common.

VERB + PARTICLE
breakdown

have a *breakdown* while driving your car	literal
have a nervous *breakdown*	transferred

throwaway

a *throwaway* razor	literal
a *throwaway* remark	transferred

PARTICLE + VERB
intake

the air *intake* on a car	literal
a new *intake* of students	transferred

outstanding

an *outstanding* performance (excellent)	literal
an *outstanding* invoice (unpaid)	transferred

I decided to treat myself to a new outfit, including new shoes, to go on holiday.

22 Nouns beginning with *out*

Nouns can be made from phrasal verbs, e.g. *overspill* from *to spill over*.
Complete the following sentences with a noun beginning with *out* plus one of
the verbs from the box.

break	burst	cast	come	cry	~~fit~~	lay	let	look	set

1 I decided to treat myself to a new out *fit*_____ , including new
shoes, to go on holiday.

2 'And now the weather forecast. Today, there will be rain
everywhere. The out_____ for the weekend: more rain.'

3 An out_____ of typhoid has been reported.

4 A shop is a retail out_____ for manufactured goods.

5 Apart from the initial out_____ on equipment, it cost us very
little to set up our business.

6 Suddenly, Tom lost his temper and started screaming and
swearing. Everyone was shocked by his out_____ .

7 There has been a huge public out_____ against the proposal
to demolish the village church.

8 A man rejected by his own people is an out_____ .

9 We are still waiting to hear the out_____ of the government
enquiry into the rail disaster.

10 Everyone knew from the out_____ that the plan would not
work.

Nouns having the pattern PARTICLE + VERB are written as one word, as
in *outbreak*.

23 Complete the caption 1

Complete the caption beside each picture using nouns made from the following verbs and particles.

VERBS:	break check hold lay tail ~~take~~
PARTICLES:	~~away~~ back by out through up

1   If you don't feel like cooking, go and get something from the Mexican __*takeaway*__ .

2   The joys of modern travel: a five-mile _____ on the freeway!

3   A non-stick frying pan! The scientific _____ we've all been waiting for!

4 It takes minutes to fill your basket, and hours to get through the supermarket _____ .

5 A bank _____ .

6 If the traffic gets too bad, pull into a _____ and have a rest.

Nouns having the pattern VERB + PARTICLE may be written with a hyphen, e.g. *set-up*, but it is now much more usual to write them as one word, e.g. *setup*, especially with very common terms, and when the verb has only one syllable.

24 Match the definitions

All these words are nouns or adjectives formed from phrasal verbs. Each one has two meanings. Match each word with the correct pair of definitions. Then try to use each one in a sentence of your own.

breakdown	fallout	~~handout~~	holdup	make-up
mixed-up	outfit	outlook	standby	take-off

1 _____ *handout* _____

something given as an act of charity, e.g. money to a beggar
or
a document containing information, often given by teachers to their students

2 _____

mentally confused
or
all grouped together, not in separate categories

3 _____

a delay caused by traffic during a very busy time
or
a robbery from a bank

4 _____

the view you have from your house
or
what you think the future might bring

5 _____

lipstick, powder, mascara, etc., to beautify the face

or

a person's nature or temperament

6 _____

an analysis of figures by an accountant

or

the situation where a car or other machine has stopped working

7 _____

the results or consequences of an action

or

specifically, the radioactive cloud after an atomic explosion

8 _____

an organisation or company

or

a set of matching clothes

9 _____

the moment when a plane leaves the ground

or

an amusing imitation of how someone behaves

10 _____

waiting to see if there are any spare seats on an aeroplane

or

something you keep handy to use in an emergency

 Always think first of the phrasal verb from which the noun or adjective has been formed, e.g. *break out* leads to *outbreak*. This will often give you a clue as to the meaning of the noun or adjective.

25 Find the definition

Choose the correct definition a, b, c or d for each of the following nouns.

1 *Grown-ups* are

a) clothes which used to belong to your older brother or sister
b) mature trees which should be cut down before they fall down
c) adult people, such as parents
d) lumps which grow on the backs of people's necks

2 A *flyover* is

a) a road bridge built over another road to make the traffic move faster
b) a lot of mosquitoes or other biting insects
c) a stage curtain in a theatre
d) a non-stop journey

3 If you are on *standby*, it means that you

a) are waiting in a long queue to go to the toilet
b) are watching other people doing something, such as fighting or playing football, without joining in yourself
c) have been abandoned by your lover, and are hoping to find another
d) haven't reserved a place on an aeroplane flight, but are waiting in case there is a spare seat

4 The word *leftovers* could describe

a) arm movements in swimming
b) the remains of a meal
c) socialists with extremist opinions
d) girls that nobody wants to dance with

5 A *dropout* is

a) a person who abandons education or career to lead a different life
b) a lump of bread or other food which you find on the floor after a messy eater has finished a meal
c) a piece of litter, such as an empty polystyrene cup or a sweet wrapper, thrown from a moving car
d) the ugly fold of flesh that hangs over a fat man's belt

50 Section 4: Nouns and adjectives formed from phrasal verbs

6 The word *stopover* is used to describe

a) someone who stays too long at a party

b) a place you stay at to break a long journey

c) the highest note you can play on a musical instrument

d) a common stomach problem that people get when they go on holiday

7 A *drawback* is

a) a drawing of someone done on the back of an envelope

b) a refund of money to someone who has paid too much tax

c) the act of reversing a car round a corner

d) a disadvantage in a plan

8 A *tip-off* is

a) something that has fallen off the back of a truck

b) information about a crime given to the police

c) a word to describe the problems of a very short person

d) the act of raising your hat to a lady

9 A *setback* is

a) something which happens, such as a delay, to spoil your plans

b) a house which is a long way from the main road

c) in chess, returning a piece to the square it came from

d) a pain caused by standing for a long time in one position

10 A *toss-up* is

a) the way a bed looks in the morning when you have slept very badly

b) a way of wishing someone a happy birthday by throwing him or her up into the air

c) a choice between two equally attractive alternatives

d) the mark left on the ceiling when someone has tried to turn over an omelette in a pan

26 Complete the caption 2

Using combinations of the following words, complete the caption beneath each picture with the correct adjective.

VERBS:	cast ~~drive~~ get knock lean lock pick pop roll slip
PARTICLES:	away down ~~in~~ off on to up

1

You can stay in your car:
this is a ___*drive-in*___ movie.

2

These shoes have no laces:
they are _____ shoes.

3

This is not an aerosol
deodorant: it is a _____
deodorant.

4

The crooks used this as
a _____ vehicle.

5

This is a _____ book.

6

This is a _____ truck.

7

This is _____ clothing.

8

There is a sale on: everything at _____ prices.

9

The shop owner does not live here: it is a _____ shop.

10

This shed is not freestanding: it is a _____ shed.

 Adjectives having the pattern VERB + PARTICLE may be written as one word, e.g. *takeaway*, or hyphenated, e.g. *take-away*. Usually, the shorter and the commoner the adjective, the more likely it is to be written as one word. Tip: If you are not sure, use a hyphen!

27 Adjectives from phrasal verbs

Choose the adjective which best completes each sentence. As a follow-up exercise, see if you can use the others in sentences of your own.

1 Outside the town, the speed limit is 70 mph. In ___*built-up*___ areas, the speed limit is reduced to 30 mph.

   a) made-up   b) packed-up   c) built-up   d) filled-in

2 An industrial society which makes goods that are not designed to last is known as a _____ society.

   a) fallout   b) takeaway   c) set-aside   d) throwaway

3 A neglected part of a city is called a _____ area.

   a) washed-out   b) leftover   c) cast-off   d) run-down

4 Someone who is mentally confused can be described as a _____ person.

   a) cast-off   b) mixed-up   c) patched-up   d) broken-down

5 A very old carpet could be described as a _____ carpet.

   a) throwaway   b) worn-out   c) written-off   d) used-up

6 If you think and behave as if you are better than everyone else, people may describe you as a _____ person.

   a) wound-up   b) dressed-up   c) pop-up   d) stuck-up

7 After a lesson or a course, the teacher may give you additional tasks to do. These are known as _____ activities.

   a) follow-up   b) stick-on   c) workout   d) standby

8 A blouse that is transparent is called a _____ blouse.

   a) look-in   b) peepshow   c) offbeat   d) see-through

9 When one company tries to gain control of another by offering a high price for its shares, it is making a _____ bid.

   a) breakthrough   b) showdown   c) makeup   d) takeover

10 A person who is rather reserved or cold in behaviour can be described as a _____ person.

   a) stand-offish   b) stuck-up   c) overdrawn   d) outcast

28 Words and pictures

Write each word or expression from the box under the correct picture.

| a handout | a hangover | ~~a lean-to~~ | a lie in |
| make-up | a pick-up | a pinup | a showdown |

1 *a lean-to*

2 _____

3 _____

4 _____

5 _____

6 _____

7 _____

8 _____

Section 5:
Three-part phrasal verbs

The pattern VERB + PREPOSITION is quite common, e.g. *look for*. In some cases the verb itself might be in two parts, i.e. it might be a phrasal verb consisting of VERB + ADVERB (e.g. *look up*). When a preposition (e.g. *to*) is added, this gives a so-called three-part phrasal verb (*look up to*). Three-part phrasal verbs always have the pattern VERB + ADVERB + PREPOSITION.

The commonest adverb particles used in these three-part phrasals are *up*, *out*, *in* and *down*. The commonest prepositions used are *with*, *on*, *to* and *for*.

Of course, the object always follows the preposition, e.g. *I like to look back on **my childhood***.

It's rude to drop in on other people's conversation. It's called 'eavesdropping'.

29 Mix and match 1

Join each phrasal verb in Column A with a word or phrase from Column B to give a common expression. Then match the verbs in Column A with the correct definitions in Column C.

Column A

1	come in for...	_d_
2	go in for...	___
3	sit in on...	___
4	stand in for...	___
5	fall in with...	___
6	give in to...	___
7	tune in to...	___
8	listen in on...	___
9	cash in on...	___
10	drop in on...	___

Column B

a	...another teacher's lesson
b	...temptation
c	...an opportunity
d	...a lot of criticism
e	...friends
f	...a sport or hobby
g	...other people's conversation
h	...somebody else's plans
i	...an absent colleague
j	...a programme on the radio

Column C

i	listen to	_7_
ii	replace	___
iii	observe	___
iv	take advantage of	___
v	not resist	___
vi	visit	___
vii	receive	___
viii	show support for	___
ix	practise	___
x	eavesdrop	___

It is a good idea to learn three-part phrasal verbs as part of a complete expression. So, for example, don't just learn *come up against*; learn *come up against a difficulty*.
Note: The commonest combinations with *in* are *in on* and *in for*.

30 Complete the caption 3

Complete the cartoon captions using the words in the box (adverb + preposition).

~~back to~~   behind with   up for   out against   out of   out on

---

1   'OK, everybody. Tea break over. Time to get _back_ _to_ work!'

2   'We speak _____ _____ injustice wherever we find it.'

3   'The problem is that we've run _____ _____ matches.'

4 'My wife has walked
_____ _____ me.
I can't think why.'

5 'Please don't wait
_____ _____ me.'

6 'This is what happens when
you fall _____
_____ the rent.'

31 Three-part phrasal verbs

Complete each sentence using the correct phrasal verb from the box.

---

catch up with	~~come up against~~	cut down on
get down to	give in to	listen in on	look up to
look forward to	put up with	run out of

---

1 We wanted to buy an apartment near Pacific Beach, but we seem to have _come_ _up_ _against_ a real problem: we can't get a bank loan.

2 You have done nothing for weeks and your exams are only a week away. It really is time for you to _____ _____ _____ some serious study.

3 I would make you an omelette, but unfortunately we have _____ _____ _____ eggs.

4 My doctor says caffeine is bad for me, so I have to _____ _____ _____ the number of cups of coffee I drink every day.

5 What is a 'role model'? It is someone you _____ _____ _____, that is, someone you really admire and want to be like.

6 If parents always _____ _____ _____ their children's wishes, the children are likely to become spoiled.

7 You live near an airport, so there's no point in complaining about low-flying aircraft over your house. You just have to _____ _____ _____ the noise.

8 It's rude to _____ _____ _____ other people's conversation. It's called 'eavesdropping'.

9 I know the party starts at eight, darling, but I just have to finish off this piece of work first. You go on ahead and I will _____ _____ _____ you later.

10 Dear Sir

Please tell me why you have not sent me the money you owe me.

I _____ _____ _____ hearing from you.

Yours faithfully

'I know the party starts at eight, darling, but I just have to finish off this piece of work first. You go on ahead.'

Always think of the three-part phrasal verb as a single verb followed by its object, e.g. **come up against** a difficulty is the same as **encounter** a difficulty.

32 Complete the caption 4

Complete the cartoon captions using the words in the box (adverb + preposition).

~~away for~~   away with   down to   forward to   on about   out of

---

1 'SEND __*away*__ __*for*__ YOUR COPY TODAY! ONLY TWENTY-FIVE DOLLARS!'

2 'What it really boils _____ _____, then, is that you don't love me any more. Is that it?'

3 'You'll never get _____ _____ it!'

4 Not everyone looks

_____ _____

Christmas.

5 'Don't worry, he's just a
puppy. He'll soon grow

_____ _____ it.'

6 'It's no good going

_____ _____ it –
you lost, and that's all there
is to it.'

33 Mix and match 2

Join each phrasal verb in Column A with a word or phrase from Column B to give a common expression. Then match the verbs in Column A with the correct definitions in Column C.

Column A

				Column B	
1	come down with...	_i_	a	...people who are beneath you
2	cut down on...	___	b	...your specialist subject
3	look down on...	___	c	...a difficulty
4	get down to...	___	d	...expenses
5	be down to...	___	e	...your beliefs
6	be up on...	___	f	...prison
7	check up on...	___	g	...your last penny
8	end up in...	___	h	...someone's movements
9	stand up for...	___	i	...flu
10	come up against...	___	j	...some hard work

Column C

i	investigate	_7_
ii	apply yourself to	___
iii	despise	___
iv	defend	___
v	know a lot about	___
vi	meet	___
vii	catch	___
viii	have nothing else left	___
ix	reduce	___
x	finally go to	___

The verb in the three-part phrasal verb often gives you a clue to the meaning of the whole phrasal verb, as in **stand up for** *your rights*: you might literally *stand up* in a public meeting and speak about your rights. Note: The commonest combinations with *down* are *down to* and *down on*.

34 Mix and match 3

Join each phrasal verb in Column A with a word or phrase from Column B to give a common expression. Then match the verbs in Column A with the correct definitions in Column C.

Column A

1	come up to...	_c_
2	face up to...	____
3	look up to...	____
4	own up to...	____
5	stand up to...	____
6	come up with...	____
7	put up with...	____
8	catch up with...	____
9	get down to...	____
10	split up with...	____

Column B

a	...business
b	...your crimes
c	...expectations
d	...your girl/boyfriend
e	...noisy neighbours
f	...your responsibilities
g	...a good idea
h	...the car in front
i	...a bully
j	...someone you respect

Column C

i	admit to	_4_
ii	reach	____
iii	accept	____
iv	leave	____
v	start	____
vi	fulfil	____
vii	produce	____
viii	defy	____
ix	tolerate	____
x	admire	____

Note: The commonest combinations with *up* are *up to* and *up with*.

35 Word search

Find the phrasal verbs in the word search and match them with the definitions in the list. The words may be horizontal, vertical or diagonal, and they may be written backwards or forwards.

	Definition	Hint: Think of...	Phrasal verb
1	explode/inflate	a bomb, a balloon	*blow up*
2	improve	your knowledge of English	
3	demand	a reform	
4	resume (work)	the work you were doing	
5	enter	a room	
6	arise	a matter, a question	
7	forgo	a pleasure, such as candies	
8	complete	your income tax return	
9	adapt	mixing well with other people	
10	not stop	someone who talks too much	
11	admit, reveal	a secret	
12	invent	a lie, something that isn't true	
13	admit	a fault, a mistake you made	
14	withdraw	someone leaving a team or a group	
15	postpone	a tennis match when it starts to rain	
16	cheat, swindle	being charged too much for something	
17	relax	a class going quiet when the teacher enters	

18	arrive unannounced	your long-lost cousin from Patagonia!	_____
19	exhaust	a really old car engine	_____
20	deduce, solve	the answer to a crossword clue	_____

S	E	T	T	L	E	D	O	W	N	J	L
E	T	U	O	L	L	U	P	O	I	K	E
C	A	R	R	Y	O	N	A	R	L	S	T
L	L	N	F	B	S	P	N	K	L	X	O
B	R	U	S	H	U	P	D	O	I	R	N
L	U	P	S	E	Y	M	U	U	F	I	C
O	L	E	K	S	P	F	F	T	U	P	A
W	E	A	R	O	U	T	B	F	O	O	L
U	M	I	G	A	E	N	I	I	S	F	L
P	U	N	W	O	M	M	F	T	O	F	F
O	R	M	E	C	O	M	E	I	N	T	O
T	U	O	T	U	C	N	B	N	Y	E	R

Section 6: Phrasal equivalents of more formal verbs

There is a difference between informal and formal language. Informal language is used every day in ordinary conversations. Sometimes people want to be more formal. There are several reasons why people use formal language:

- to impress other people
- to make a speech
- to write something serious

For example, instead of the informal *try*, you might say *endeavour*. Phrasal verbs are part of the everyday language, and many have formal equivalents, e.g.

| INFORMAL | *fill in* a form | *put up with* a noise |
| FORMAL | *complete* a form | *tolerate* a noise |

'Don't take any notice of Ruth. She always likes to show off in front of visitors.'

36 Formal and informal 1

Replace the underlined word(s) with the phrasal verbs in the box.

brush up	clear up	come into	come round	~~go on~~
look into	make up	pull out	stand for	think over

1   Shall I <u>continue</u> painting this wall, or would you like me to do something else?   *go on*

2   If I won a lot of money, I would need to <u>consider carefully</u> how I would spend it.   _____

3   If someone faints, put their head between their knees and they will soon <u>regain consciousness</u>.   _____

4   I believe that my next-door neighbour has recently <u>inherited</u> a lot of money.   _____

5   Nobody knows yet where 'Odmedod', the latest computer virus, came from. Experts from Virus Busters have been brought in to <u>investigate</u> the incident.   _____

6   I'm glad that we have been able to <u>resolve</u> our little misunderstanding.   _____

7   I don't think the people will <u>tolerate</u> another increase in taxes.   _____

8   Switzerland had intended to enter a team for the International Tiddlywinks Contest, but had to <u>withdraw</u> at the last moment when they realised that nobody in Switzerland knew how to play the game.   _____

9   I need to <u>improve</u> my French. I learned it at school but I haven't spoken it for years.   _____

10 If you haven't got a genuine reason for being late, you'll simply have to <u>invent</u> an excuse.   _____

Often the meaning of a phrasal verb is easy to work out from the two parts, the VERB and the PARTICLE. Sometimes, though, the phrasal is an idiomatic expression, which you simply have to learn, as in *take someone off*, which means *impersonate someone*.

37 Formal and informal 2

Combine these verbs and particles to make phrasal verbs which can replace the definitions underlined in the sentences.

> VERBS: break carry clear draw fill ~~give~~ make put step turn
> PARTICLES: ~~away~~ down   forward   in   off   out   up

1   I hate people who <u>reveal</u> the end of a film that I haven't seen yet.   _give away_

2   With the introduction of computers, we have been able to <u>increase</u> production by 25 per cent.   _____

3   A soldier is expected to <u>obey</u> a superior officer's orders without question.   _____

4   Harry says he intends to <u>terminate</u> his engagement to Naomi because she always opens her boiled eggs at the wrong end.

    _____

5   It's important in a relationship to <u>resolve</u> little misunderstandings before they turn into big problems.   _____

6   Before we do anything else, we ought to <u>prepare</u> a plan of action.

    _____

7   Was that a true story about you hacking into the Pentagon computer?   No, I <u>invented</u> it!   _____

8   Our society has become so bureaucratic that you even have to <u>complete</u> a form before you are allowed to die. _____

9   As nobody seems to know what to do next, may I <u>propose</u> a solution?   _____

10 Alan is very upset. The Team Manager intends to <u>reject</u> his application to play in goal on the grounds that his legs are too thin.

    _____

When the phrasal verb consists of a verb and an adverb, where does the object go? If the object is a personal pronoun, it must come between, as in **pick** *it* **up**. If it consists of a very short phrase, it may come between, as in **pick** *the best ones* **out** (in a crowd); or after the particle, as in **pick out** *the best ones*. If the object consists of a long phrase, put it after the particle, as in **pick up** *all the books you've left lying on the floor*. When in doubt, put the object after the particle!

38 Definitions 1

Use these phrasal verbs to complete the sentences.

come round	fall off	fall out	run down	~~show up~~
split up	think over	throw away	tip off	touch on

1   To make someone look foolish or embarrass them in front of
    other people is to __show__ them ___up___ .

2   The Buddha said 'If you can't say anything good about a person,
    say nothing.' That is why I never criticise people or _____
    them _____ .

3   When two lovers quarrel, we say that they _____ _____ .

4   If the two lovers separate, we say that they _____ _____ .

5   If someone makes a suggestion to you, and you decide to consider
    it very carefully before agreeing, we say that you are going to
    _____ it _____ .

6   If you happen to mention a subject briefly, we say that you
    _____ _____ it.

7   When you know that something bad is going to happen, and you
    warn people about it, we say that you _____ them _____ .

8   If a boxer is knocked out, when he eventually regains
    consciousness, we say that he has finally _____ _____ .

9   When the number of students attending a class decreases, we say
    that attendance has started to _____ _____ .

10 When you discard something because you no longer need it, you
    _____ it _____ .

When the particle is a PREPOSITION, as in *look after*, the object always comes
after the particle, e.g. *Will you look after me when I am old and grey?* The
particles *after, at, for, from, into, to, with* and *without* are always prepositions.
The particles *away, back, forward* and *out* are always adverbs. All other
particles, e.g. *in, off, over* and *up*, may be either prepositions or adverbs.

39 Formal and informal 3

Use these verbs and particles to make phrasal verbs which can replace the formal versions underlined in the sentences.

VERBS: brush come do explain go let pick ~~settle~~ stand strip
PARTICLES: away ~~down~~ for into off on out round up without

1   Please <u>be quiet and pay attention</u>,
everybody!   *settle down*

2   Distance-learning programmes can help
you to study for a degree, or to <u>improve</u>
your knowledge of a foreign language.   _____

3   <u>Get undressed</u> and wait for the doctor.   _____

4   Do you think there is enough food to
<u>feed everybody</u>?   _____

5   I don't think the people will <u>tolerate</u>
another increase in taxes.   _____

6   A tall person is always easy to <u>distinguish</u>
in a crowd.   _____

7   If we cannot get any bread, we'll just
have to <u>manage</u>.   _____

8   All my brother's knives and forks have got
'Hotel Excelsior, Cairo' stamped on them.
I don't know how he is going to <u>convince
people that there is nothing wrong with</u>
this situation.   _____

9   Please don't <u>mention anything</u> to the
children about the party: I want it to
be a surprise.   _____

10   When Aunt Jane died, I expected to <u>inherit</u>
a fortune, but all I got was a pair of
binoculars and a stuffed owl.   _____

40 Definitions 2

Using the verbs and particles given, make up phrasal verbs which complete the definitions of the words in italics.

> VERBS: blow call carry ~~out~~ fit set shake slip wear work
>
> PARTICLES: ~~down~~ for in off on out up

1 If you decide to *reduce* the amount of food you eat, we say that you have decided to ___*cut*___ ___*down*___ .

2 To *embark on a journey* is to _____ _____.

3 To *destroy a bridge using explosive* is to _____ it _____.

4 When people *demand* something, for example, a change in the law, we say that they _____ _____ a change.

5 After a long time and lot of use, a machine may *no longer function properly*. We say that it has started to _____ _____.

6 To *commit an error* is to _____ _____.

7 To *deduce* the answer to a problem is to _____ _____ the answer.

8 To *continue* doing something is to _____ _____ doing it.

9 If you *recover easily and quickly* from a cold, we say that you were able to _____ _____ your cold.

10 If new people join an established group and they *quickly become accepted*, we say that they were able to _____ _____ very well.

41 Formal and informal 4

Using the following verbs and particles, make phrasal verbs which mean the same as the formal word or expression in capital letters. In some cases, you will need to change the tense or form of the verb.

VERBS: ~~drop~~ get give look play pull put turn

PARTICLES: away down ~~in~~ off out of through up

---

1 ARRIVE UNANNOUNCED

I just __*dropped*__ ____*in*____ to wish you a Merry Christmas!

2 ARRIVE CASUALLY

John is not very punctual. He usually _____ _____ ten minutes after the lesson has started.

3 MINIMISE THE IMPORTANCE

After the accident at the nuclear power station, the authorities tried to _____ _____ the danger to the public from radioactivity.

4 WITHDRAW FROM

A number of people had to _____ _____ the New York Marathon because they were just not fit enough to complete the distance.

5 POSTPONE

Because of the heavy rains during the week, the match, which was to take place on Saturday, has been _____ _____ until next Wednesday.

6 ABANDON

Robert Brent has _____ _____ his attempt to beat
the record for eating hard-boiled eggs, because he is afraid of
getting salmonella.

7 SCRUTINISE/REVIEW

Several people _____ _____ the draft report, but
there were still a number of spelling mistakes in the final version.

8 ESCAPE

The police chased the thieves for several miles but the thieves
managed to _____ _____ because their car was
faster.

9 LEAVE

If we can manage to _____ _____ from the office
early enough, we intend to go to the theatre.

42 Crazy headlines 1

Underline the spelling mistake in each of these newspaper headlines.

1

DR MARTEN'S BOYS TOLD: '<u>LACE</u> UP TO YOUR RESPONSIBILITIES'

2

MAN ADMITS TO KNIFE ATTACK ON NOISY NEIGHBOURS: 'IT WAS IMPOSSIBLE TO CUT UP WITH THEM ANY MORE,' HE SAYS.

3

PEOPLE IN BIG CARS ALWAYS TRY TO MATCH UP WITH THE CAR IN FRONT

4

SCUBA DIVER 'DRIPPED IN' ON SUBMARINE. 'I JUST WANTED TO SAY HELLO.'

5

OVERPRICED HAIRDRESSERS COMB IN FOR A LOT OF CRITICISM

6

OUTBREAK OF MYSTERY ILLNESS AMONGST POULTRY. MINISTRY OF AGRICULTURE PROMISES TO CHICK UP ON IT.

7

HOW TO STAY CALM: CUP DOWN ON THE AMOUNT OF COFFEE YOU DRINK!

8

ECONOMISTS PREDICT BIG INCREASE IN POTATO SALES. FARMERS ADVISED TO MASH IN ON THIS OPPORTUNITY

9

STOP COMPARING YOURSELF WITH YOUR NEIGHBOUR, ADVISES SOCIAL WORKER: 'USELESS TO TRY TO PEEP UP WITH THE JONESES'

10

POST OFFICE PROMISES BETTER MAIL DELIVERY: 'HAPPY TO CALL IN WITH CUSTOMERS' WISHES'

Section 7:
Phrasal verbs in context

This section is about deducing (working out) the meaning of a phrasal verb even when you don't know the verb. Each sentence gives you a context, that is, each sentence describes a situation which gives you a clue as to the meaning of the phrasal verb. This is, indeed, how we learn new words and expressions in our own language. For example, suppose you hear the sentence: 'Please speak clearly. When you *grurple*, I can't understand a word you are saying.' You haven't heard the word *grurple* before (there is no such word!), but you can deduce that it means something like *mumble* or *speak indistinctly*.

Remember, too, that the particle in a phrasal verb also carries part of the meaning.

Mrs Milton has forty-three cats. I don't know how she copes with them all.

43 Phrasal verbs in context 1

Choose the phrasal verb which best completes the sentence.

1 Dad, I'm sorry to ___*bring*___ ___*up*___ the matter again, but I really need to have a computer of my own now that I'm preparing for my final exams.

a) set forth   b) call out
c) bring up   d) hint at

2 Chico is a strange man: I cannot _____ him _____.

a) make out   b) string along
c) root out   d) spur on

3 It's no use _____ _____ the children when they are naughty. It only makes them worse!

a) blowing up   b) shouting at
c) running into   d) putting off

4 I'm sorry, but I don't think you and I have met before. Are you sure you're not _____ me _____ with somebody else?

a) pairing off   b) putting together
c) fitting in   d) mixing up

5 I couldn't remember where I had left my car, when it suddenly _____ _____ me that I didn't have a car!

a) dawned on   b) ran into
c) went through   d) tumbled to

6 That's the third time you've asked me where I got the money to buy my car. I'm not sure what you're _____ _____, but I didn't steal the money, if that's what you mean!

a) coming to   b) working on
c) making up   d) getting at

7 The subject of human rights seems to _____ _____ in every discussion lesson in my school.

a) burst out   b) zero in
c) crop up   d) harp on

8 Whole villages have been _____ _____ by the floods.

a) wiped out   b) mopped up
c) called off   d) run down

9 The business had been allowed to _____ _____ to such an extent that it was sold for only a quarter of its true market value.

a) tail off   b) fade away
c) play out   d) run down

10 Ruth wanted to go to Cyprus or Rhodes, her husband Peter wanted to go to Scotland or Ireland. In the end they _____ _____ Cyprus.

a) hit on   b) jumped at
c) plumped for   d) plunged into

Note: Sometimes all the options (a, b, c and d) will fit in some way, but only one really makes sense in the context. For example, in 3, it is possible to *blow up* the children, *run into* them or *put* them *off!* But the only option that makes sense is *shouting at*.

44 Phrasal verbs in context 2

Choose the phrasal verb which best completes the sentence.

1 Simon never takes anything seriously. He just likes _fooling_ _around_ .

a) splashing out   b) acting up

c) fooling around   d) playing along

2 'Is it raining?'
'Raining? It's absolutely _____ _____!'

a) pouring down   b) streaming away

c) spurting out   d) flooding in

3 It is a serious operation for a woman as old as my grandmother. She's very frail. I hope she _____ _____.

a) gets away   b) comes round

c) pulls through   d) stands up

4 This message is in very bad handwriting. I can't _____ it _____.

a) make out   b) put in

c) bring off   d) carry on

5 Charlie had such bad stomach ache that he was _____ _____ with pain.

a) bent down   b) folded over

c) doubled up   d) snapped off

6 'The name Cindy keeps _____ _____ in conversation. Who on earth is Cindy?'

'Isn't that your wife's name, sir?'

a) bursting out   b) slipping by

c) cropping up   d) harping on

7 The crowd was so angry that it took their leaders ages to get them to _____ _____.

a) peter out   b) sober up

c) simmer down   d) whittle away

8 The factory is now fully automated, which means that we have been able to _____ _____ production.

a) run on   b) step up

c) turn over   d) double up

9 Why don't you try praising your students occasionally instead of _____ _____ them all the time?

a) crying to   b) shouting at

c) rushing into   d) falling over

10 When I got into trouble, all my friends deserted me. My best friend was the only person who _____ _____ me.

a) stuck by   b) stood for

c) held to   d) leant on

 Look up new words in a dictionary, but don't be surprised if the verb does not have its literal meaning as it is used in the phrasal verb. For example, a *crop* is *something that grows or comes up out of the ground*, from which we get the phrasal verb to *crop up* in the sense of *something that is mentioned (comes up) in conversation*.

45 Choose the verb

In each sentence, choose the verb that best fits.

1   'Are you ill? You look terrible!'
    'Well, I am a bit ___*run*___ down. The doctor says I must rest.'

    a) run   b) turned   c) knocked

2   Some people can just _____ off a cold, but mine last for ages.

    a) shrug   b) wash   c) slide

3   Isn't this terrible weather for April! _____ on summer!'

    a) Roll   b) Call   c) Drag

4   I just want to _____ myself up a bit before we go out to
    dinner.

    a) freshen   b) liven   c) touch

5   You must be _____ me up with someone else. I am NOT an
    actor!

    a) mixing   b) matching   c) pairing

6   Poor Malcolm was completely taken in for a while. He'll never be
    able to _____ it down.

    a) live   b) hold   c) keep

7   If you never put oil in your engine, one day it will _____ up
    completely.

    a) seize   b) shut   c) crash

8 When he ran off with the company funds, the Board tried to
_____ up the whole affair.

a) hush   b) close   c) tuck

---

9 I was at a party, and people kept staring at me. Then it _____
on me: I was at the wrong party!

a) dawned   b) hit   c) shone

---

10 I have a busy day tomorrow, so I think I'll _____ in now.
Good night!

a) turn   b) lie   c) lay

46 Phrasal verbs in context 3

Choose the phrasal verb which best completes the sentence.

1 Teachers tend to ___skate___ ___over___ certain subjects that they find difficult to talk about.

a) boil down   b) string along
c) skate over   d) track down

2 The new office block _____ _____ well with its surroundings.

a) blends in   b) stands out
c) shaped up   d) sets off

3 Whole villages have been _____ _____ by the floods.

a) wiped out   b) mopped up
c) called off   d) run down

4 You may not like what has happened but you cannot simply _____ _____. It really happened, and you must face up to that fact.

a) dream up   b) wish away
c) run away   d) tone down

5 It's a good idea to _____ _____ people before taking them into your confidence.

a) tumble to   b) root out
c) bank on   d) size up

6 Mrs Milton has forty-three cats. I don't know how she _____ _____ them all.

a) looks for   b) stands by
c) keeps to   d) copes with

7 'Have you any plans for the summer vacation?'

'I'm glad you _____ _____ the subject. I was thinking of getting a job as a windsurfing instructor.'

a) set forth   b) called out

c) brought up   d) hinted at

8 When the dentist has finished drilling the bad parts from your tooth, she will offer you a glass of peculiar pink liquid and tell you to _____ your mouth _____.

a) brush off   b) wash up

c) rinse out   d) scrub down

9 Unfortunately, somebody spoke to a reporter, and the whole thing _____ _____.

a) poured forth   b) spilled over

c) leaked out   d) splashed down

10 I don't know whether Sabrina and her husband would be interested in joining our Conservation Society. I'll _____ them _____ about it.

a) chat up   b) sound out

c) tell off   d) spur on

47 Which one doesn't fit?

In each of the sentences 1 to 5, underline the **three** verbs that are correct.
Then complete sentences a to e on page 87 with the verbs you didn't use.
In some cases, you will need to change the tense or form of the verb.

1   My father doesn't approve of the people I a) go   around with.
                                                    b) hang
                                                    c) play
                                                    d) knock

2   When people panic, they usually a) lash out at the nearest person.
                                                    b) strike
                                                  c) hit
                                                  d) rush

3   I've had to a) hold out for four new tyres for my car.
                  b) fork
                  c) shell
                  d) pay

4   If you're not careful, you'll a) stock up with a face like mine.
                                    b) end
                                    c) land
                                    d) finish

5   'Why don't you come round to our place for a drink one night?'
    'Tell you what, I'll a) butt in on you on the way home.'
                                    b) drop
                                    c) look
                                    d) call

a   _____ out for the result you want.

b   I didn't mean to _____ in on your conversation, but I couldn't help overhearing my name mentioned.

c   When the pop star left the theatre, all his fans _____ out at him.

d   I was just _____ around with this digital camera when I dropped it. Luckily it wasn't damaged.

e   Are you expecting bad weather? Do you always _____ up with enough food to last you six months?

'My father doesn't approve of the people I hang around with.'

Remember: Three of the choices are correct; one is not. For example, two people are having a conversation about the crime rate. They are *speaking* about it, *talking* about it, *chatting* about it or *minding* about it. The first three (*speak, talk, chat*) fit, but the fourth one (*mind*) doesn't.

48 Phrasal verbs in context 4

Choose the phrasal verb which best completes the sentence.

1 The interrogation seemed to _____drag_____ _____on_____ for ages, but in fact it only lasted twenty minutes.

a) fritter away   (b) drag on
c) spin off   d) play out

2 It's none of your business: please don't _____ _____ things that don't concern you.

a) bump into   b) meddle with
c) tot up   d) come across

3 'He's only a mailman, but he has just bought a brand new Cadillac. I wonder how he can afford it.'
'I can see what you're _____ _____ . You think he might be a crook, right?'

a) coming to   b) working on
c) making up   d) getting at

4 'That was a very dirty trick you played on your colleagues.'
'I know. I feel badly enough about it as it is. You don't need to _____ it _____ .'

a) turn on   b) clamp down
c) stick up   d) rub in

5 The man in the market was selling leather coats very cheaply: they were such bargains that they were soon _____ _____ .

a) cleared of   b) done for
c) bought out   d) snapped up

6 I was so tired that I just _____ _____ in the armchair.

a) flaked out   b) broke up
c) dropped out   d) fell over

---

7 I always wanted to be an actor, so when they offered me a part as the back end of a pantomime horse, I _____ _____ the chance!

a) burst into   b) seized on
c) ran after   d) jumped at

---

8 It's really hard work trying to find the right Smith in the London telephone directory: you may have to _____ _____ about thirty pages of Smiths.

a) wade through   b) rip out
c) tramp across   d) peer at

---

9 I watched a very old professor giving a lecture the other day. He _____ _____ for ages before getting to the point.

a) rambled on   b) ran forward
c) went ahead   d) circled round

---

10 When we won some money on the lottery, I wanted to buy a new car but my partner wanted to spend it on a holiday. After a lot of discussion, we _____ _____ the holiday.

a) came to   b) plumped for
c) agreed with   d) jumped on

49 Proverbs

Complete each of these well-known proverbs with the correct phrasal verb.
Then, match each proverb with the correct picture.

~~bite off~~	come out	look after	pick up
put off	run away	throw out	turn over

1. Don't __bite__ __off__ more than you can chew.

2. Don't _____ _____ the baby with the bath water.

3. _____ _____ a new leaf (= page).

4. Never _____ _____ till tomorrow what you can do today.

5. _____ _____ the pennies and the pounds will _____ _____ themselves.

6. The sun always _____ _____ after the rain.

7. He who fights and _____ _____ ,
Lives to fight another day.

8. See a pin and _____ it _____,
And all day long you'll have good luck.

A

Don't bite off more than you can chew.

B

_____

_____

_____

_____

_____

_____

_____

_____

_____

_____

_____

_____

_____

_____

Section 8: Phrasal verbs in idiomatic expressions

Phrasal verbs occur in many idiomatic expressions. Sometimes you can guess the meaning from the verb and/or the particle, e.g. *dry* means *there is no water*, and *up* can mean *completely*. Literally, a lake might *dry up*. When someone is making a speech but then cannot think of what to say next, we can say that that person has *dried up* – there are no more words, just as there is no more water in the lake.

Sometimes, though, you need to guess the meaning from the context. For example, in the sentence *It's raining now but it should **clear up** later on*, the word *but* tells you that the rain will stop soon. So, *clear up* must mean something like *stop raining*.

Anna loves tinkering with old sports cars.

50 Phrasal verbs in idiomatic expressions 1

Choose the alternative which best matches the meaning of the phrasal verb in capitals.

1 In London this morning, three people wearing masks HELD UP a van carrying gold bullion.

a) robbed
b) lifted
c) delayed
d) stole

2 The nurse is on a case right now, but he can probably FIT you IN later on.

a) examine
b) try to cure
c) find time to see
d) look after

3 She had such a bad cold that I was not surprised she DOZED OFF in the middle of the afternoon.

a) forgot to take her medicine
b) fell asleep
c) felt very ill
d) went home early

4 It was so hot in the theatre that I almost DROPPED OFF.

a) decided to leave
b) fell from the balcony
c) fainted
d) fell asleep

5 Don't buy the first thing you see: SHOP AROUND a bit.

a) visit many shops to compare prices
b) find the cheapest one
c) look at everything in the shop
d) decide exactly what you want

6 It was getting late so I decided to TURN IN.

a) give up
b) go to bed
c) switch off the light
d) go home

7 What terrible weather! Do you think the rain will EASE OFF soon?

a) get worse
b) turn to snow
c) lessen
d) stay the same

8 The London-to-Sydney flight TOUCHED DOWN IN Bombay.

a) made a stop at
b) crashed in
c) flew low over
d) was forced to land in

9 I wonder who first HIT UPON the idea of using invisible ink to send secret messages.

a) finally rejected
b) carefully developed
c) openly criticised
d) suddenly thought of

10 My speech started well, but I DRIED UP after a few minutes.

a) got bored
b) couldn't continue
c) decided to cut it short
d) began to feel thirsty

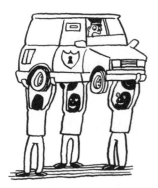 

*In London this morning, three people wearing masks HELD UP
a van carrying gold bullion.*

 You need always to distinguish between the literal and the non-literal (idiomatic) use of phrasal verbs. For example, the cartoon shows the two possible meanings of the sentence *They held up a van carrying gold bullion.*

51 Phrasal verbs in idiomatic expressions 2

Choose the alternative which best matches the meaning of the phrasal verb in capitals.

1 Janet is very upset. I'd like you to try and SMOOTH things OVER if you can.

a) tidy the place up for her   b) calm her down

c) tell her not to be silly   d) hide the truth from her

2 Jamie needs a place to stay? I can PUT him UP here.

a) give him some money   b) send him away

c) let him stay here   d) recommend a good hostel

3 They had a quarrel one evening, but they PATCHED things UP next morning.

a) hid their feelings   b) repaired the furniture

c) continued to quarrel   d) settled their differences

4 I knew exactly what she wanted me to do: she didn't need to SPELL it OUT for me.

a) tell me how to write it down   b) help me to do it

c) explain it any further   d) plan my life for me

5 Bill had to DIP INTO his savings account to pay for his holiday.

a) increase   b) close

c) take money from   d) put money into

6 It was so hot in the examination room that several students NODDED OFF.

a) left the room   b) started arguing

c) fell asleep   d) fainted

7 I think we should WIND UP the discussion now: it's getting late and we have to be up early in the morning.

   a) postpone   b) end

   c) cancel   d) restrict

8 My father TOLD me OFF because I used his electric razor.

   a) reprimanded me   b) was proud of me

   c) laughed at me   d) congratulated me

9 Andy wanted to go to the ball, so poor Anne had to COUGH UP fifty pounds for the tickets.

   a) reluctantly pay out   b) easily save up

   c) confidently ask for   d) unwillingly borrow

10 I need twenty pounds to TIDE me OVER until the end of the month.

   a) cover my expenses   b) pay off my debts

   c) spend   d) borrow

'My father told me off because I used his electric razor.'

52 Phrasal verbs in idiomatic expressions 3

Choose the alternative which best matches the meaning of the phrasal verb in capitals.

1 The police officer SHOT OFF before anyone could stop her.

a) left in a hurry   b) told everyone the truth
c) fired her gun   d) closed all the doors

2 The teacher told her students to stop MESSING ABOUT, especially now that their examinations were only two weeks away.

a) bringing food to the class   b) coming late all the time
c) being absent from class   d) wasting time

3 The doctor is busy right now, but she could probably FIT you IN later on.

a) examine you   b) try to cure you
c) find time to see you d) send you away

4 Have you managed to TRACK DOWN that book I asked you about?

a) sell   b) read through
c) find   d) get back

5 He had no business there, so I told him to CLEAR OFF.

a) do the dishes   b) leave at once
c) put everything in its place   d) find something useful to do

6   I'm sorry to BUTT IN, but I couldn't help overhearing what you said.

a) interrupt you   b) contradict you
c) speak so rudely to you   d) refuse you

7   As it was getting late, I decided to PRESS ON.

a) find a place to sleep   b) phone for help
c) finish the ironing   d) keep going

8   I knew that nobody would help me, so I decided to SOLDIER ON.

a) let someone else do the work b) continue by myself
c) abandon the job   d) join the army

9   I get up very early in the morning, so I am ready to TURN IN by about 8 pm!

a) give up   b) go to bed
c) switch off the light   d) go home

10   I didn't want to do it, but the other boys EGGED me ON.

a) threw eggs at me   b) called me names
c) encouraged me   d) lifted me off the ground

53 Phrasal verbs in idiomatic expressions 4

Choose the alternative which best matches the meaning of the phrasal verb in capitals.

1 If you got up earlier, you wouldn't need to BOLT your breakfast DOWN.

a) miss your breakfast   b) eat your breakfast very quickly

c) go without breakfast   d) make your own breakfast

2 The war in Hernia seems to be DRAGGING ON.

a) coming to an end   b) involving more and more people

c) getting worse   d) continuing indefinitely

3 If you spend half the night on the internet, it's not surprising if you DOZE OFF in class!

a) forget where you are   b) fall asleep

c) feel very ill   d) forget to take your medicine

4 She looked really WASHED OUT after her operation.

a) very clean   b) soaking wet

c) very tired and pale   d) very untidy

5 It is snowing heavily at the moment, but it is expected to EASE OFF later.

a) stay the same   b) freeze

c) move away   d) lessen

6 Joanna managed to SCRAPE THROUGH her final examinations.

a) arrive late for   b) barely pass

c) stay awake during   d) just fail

7 I know Sam said he would lend you some money, but I wouldn't BANK ON it if I were you.

a) borrow from him   b) spend the money all at once

c) save the money   d) depend on him to do it

---

8 Mail is PILING UP at all the main sorting offices because of the postal strike.

a) not being posted   b) getting lost

c) accumulating   d) being put into large boxes

---

9 You must try not to DWELL ON your brother's problems.

a) think too much about   b) forget

c) benefit from   d) remember

---

10 We TARTED UP the house in order to be able to sell it quickly.

a) offered it at a low price

b) advertised it widely

c) decorated it cheaply and quickly

d) refurnished it

'If you got up earlier, you wouldn't need to bolt your breakfast down.'

54 Phrasal verbs in idiomatic expressions 5

Choose the alternative which best matches the meaning of the phrasal verb in capitals.

1 'Susan said I was the nicest man she had ever met. Do you think she's in love with me?'
'I wouldn't READ too much INTO her words if I were you. She says that to every man she meets!'

a) interpret her
b) try to understand her
c) make sense of her
d) take her too seriously

2 'My teacher says if you hold a guinea pig by its tail, its eyes will fall out.'
'She's HAVING you ON! Guinea pigs don't have tails!'

a) being friendly with you
b) teasing you
c) making you angry
d) trying to please you

3 Traffic on the main Interstate out of El Paso was HELD UP for three hours because of a serious accident.

a) delayed
b) diverted
c) returned
d) expected

4 'I answered an advertisement which said: Send me ten pounds and I will tell you how to get rich.'
'Oh, how could you FALL FOR that old trick!'

a) take advantage of
b) get into trouble with
c) let yourself be persuaded by
d) misunderstand

5 'Is your flight to San Diego non-stop?'
'No, it TOUCHES DOWN IN Phoenix.'

a) makes a stop at   b) stays in
c) flies low over   d) is forced to land in

---

6 Everyone agreed the old program was not user-friendly. Finally, the company HIT UPON the idea of installing this new one in all our computers.

a) finally rejected   b) suddenly thought of
c) openly criticised   d) carefully developed

---

7 'May I ask you a question?'
'FIRE AWAY!'

a) Don't worry! There's no danger   b) No!
c) Go ahead!   d) Please leave me alone!

---

8 I was so late this morning that I hardly had time to GULP DOWN a cup of tea.

a) spill   b) leave unfinished
c) make myself   d) drink quickly

---

9 My older sisters were going on a picnic, and they said that I could TAG ALONG.

a) pay for the drinks   b) walk behind them
c) go with them   d) carry the picnic basket

---

10 Why is it that Christopher always WRIGGLES OUT OF doing the washing-up?

a) gets paid for   b) avoids
c) complains about   d) never seems to mind

55 Definitions 3

Choose the alternative which best matches the meaning of the phrase in capitals.

1 At first, the Managing Director insisted that she was right and everyone else was mistaken, but in the end she was forced to CLIMB DOWN.

a) apologise   (b) admit that she was wrong
c) join in the discussion   d) resign as managing director

2 'What did the security guards say to you?'
'They told me to CLEAR OFF.'

a) go away   b) tidy the place up
c) finish my work   d) push the boat into the water

3 Simon hasn't got a job, and isn't trying to get one: he just SPONGES OFF his friends.

a) works with them   b) complains to them
c) borrows money from them   d) takes advantage of them

4 Anna loves TINKERING WITH old sports cars.

a) taking people out in   b) driving fast in
c) buying and selling   d) trying to repair

5 Rioting in the capital was SPARKED OFF by the arrest of the rebel leader.

a) prevented   b) caused
c) delayed   d) exploded

6 I was not a success as a door-to-door salesperson. The first house I went to, a man opened the door and told me to BUZZ OFF.

a) stop ringing the doorbell   b) shut up
c) try to be more interesting   d) go away and leave him alone

7 My cousins are always HARKING BACK TO the time when they were in the army.

a) complaining about   b) telling us about

c) arguing about   d) telling lies about

8 When the German army occupied Norway during the Second World War, many people refused to KNUCKLE UNDER.

a) submit to them   b) stand up to them

c) pay their taxes   d) shake hands with them

9 Some conference speakers have very little to say, but they're still able to SPIN OUT their material.

a) change the subject   b) remember their words

c) make it seem important   d) make it last a long time

10 The boss sometimes lets her staff KNOCK OFF at four o'clock.

a) hand in their work   b) stop for a tea break

c) leave work   d) make suggestions

Section 9:
Just for fun!

This section consists of two crossword puzzles and three crazy headline puzzles. With a couple of exceptions, all of the phrasal verbs in these puzzles have appeared in earlier tests in the book. Enjoy!

56 Crazy headlines 2

Underline the spelling mistake in each of these newspaper headlines.

1

MEAT PRICES ARE DOWN AGAIN. HOUSEWIVES ADVISED TO <u>CHOP</u> AROUND FOR THE BEST BARGAINS

2

DON'T KNICK OFF EARLY ON FRIDAY AFTERNOONS, WORKERS WARNED

3

LOCAL COUNCIL TELL GRAFFITI ARTISTS TO 'FUZZ OFF'

4

NEW WEBSITE BOASTS BIGGEST ENCYCLOPAEDIA OF THE WORLD'S WINES. 'WELL WORTH SIPPING INTO,' SAY THE EXPERTS

5

SAILING IS NOW THIRD MOST POPULAR HOBBY. 'MEN LOVE TO MISS ABOUT IN BOATS,' SAYS LEISURE FIRM.

6

SWIMMER'S DEATH SHARKS OFF A SAFETY ENQUIRY

7

AMAZON EXPLORERS DECIDE TO DRESS ON DESPITE THE HEAT

8

'ATTENDANCE AT WATER POLO EVENTS DRIPPING OFF' SAYS OFFICIAL REPORT

9

IMMIGRANT WORKERS FEEL ALIENATED: HAVE A HARD TIME SITTING IN

10

EIGHTY-YEAR-OLD JUDGE CRITICISED FOR RODDING OFF DURING TRIAL. 'IF HE CAN'T STAY AWAKE, HE SHOULD RETIRE,' LAWYER COMMENTS

57 Crazy headlines 3

Underline the spelling mistake in each of these newspaper headlines.

1 FIRE BRIGADE ON ALERT AS VANDALS THREATEN TO <u>TURN</u> DOWN FARM BUILDINGS

2 BRITISH ATHLETE INTENDS TO CRY FOR NEW WORLD RECORD AT COMING COMMONWEALTH GAMES

3 NEW ZEALAND NOCTURNAL GROUND PARROT IN DANGER: 'WE MUST CONSERVE ITS HABITAT OR IT WILL DIG OUT SOON,' SAYS LEADING NATURALIST.

4 SHOCK MEDICAL REPORT: STUDENTS CRANKING UP UNDER EXAMINATION PRESSURE

5 POLICE SURROUND PRISON AS DANGEROUS CRIMINALS TRY TO FREAK OUT

6 SECURITY LIGHTENED UP AT AIRPORTS AS NEW TERRORIST CAMPAIGN BEGINS

7 AFTER FIFTEEN YEARS, HUSBAND FINALLY MUMBLES TO WIFE'S LOVER

8 MANCHESTER MAN JUMPS INTO LONG-LOST BROTHER IN NEW YORK NIGHTCLUB

9 LADY CHATTERLEY TO MARRY HER GARDENER: 'I JUST HOPE IT FORKS OUT FOR THEM,' SAY HER PARENTS

10 HOUSEWIVES TIRED OF BEING TIED TO THE KITCHEN SINK: 'THERE MUST BE MORE TO LIFE THAN LASHING UP,' THEY SAY

58 Crossword

Study the clues and complete the crossword.

Across

1 Go up one side of the mountain and _____ _____ the other side. (4,4)

4 If you want something from the mail order catalogue, you will have to _____ _____ for it. (4,3)

7 When a typhoid epidemic breaks out, we say there has been an _____ of typhoid. (8)

8 Verb used in the expression '_____ away with' meaning 'get rid of'. (2)

10 This is a phrasal verb from the game of cricket. If somebody finds you very attractive, we say that you have _____ed them _____. The verb describes the way the ball is sent to the batsman. (4,4)

13 Opposite of 'up'. (4)

14 Opposite of 'off'. (2)

15 You use this to tie up parcels. (6)

Down

1 '_____-_____' clothing is clothing which you no longer want. (4,3)

2 If you break the law, you may finally _____ up in jail. (3)

3 A method of printing. The first part of the word is the same as the particle in 4 across and 1 down. (6)

5 If you want to remember exactly what someone said, don't rely on your memory: _____ it _____. The particle here is the same word as 13 across. (4,4)

6 When you _____ on thin ice, you are in danger of going through and into deep water. (5)

9 To '_____ up' is to admit that you did something. The word is also used in the expression 'on my _____', meaning 'alone'. (3)

10 Restaurants in Wellington usually _____ up very quickly on Saturdays, so it is a good idea to phone up and reserve a table. (4)

11 The opposite of 16 down. It is also the first part of 7 across. (3)

12 When you see the train about to leave the station, you have to _____ to catch it. The same verb is used in the expression 'to _____ somebody down', meaning to criticise them or give them a bad name. (3)

16 A particle used in many phrasal verbs, such as 'turn _____', meaning to go to bed, and 'give _____', meaning to surrender. (2)

59 Double definitions crossword

The answer to each clue is a two-part phrasal verb (or a noun or adjective derived from a phrasal verb). Each clue consists of two parts. The first part gives a dictionary definition; the second gives a typical sentence in which the phrasal verb might be used. The following verbs and particles are used.

Verbs

aim	book	burn	carry	cast	fall	lie	look	make
set	sit	stand	switch	touch	turn	walk	work	

Particles

about	at	back	by	down	in	off	on	out	over	up

Across

3 Be careful, take care. (4,3)
'_____ _____! There's a car behind you!'

5 Point towards. (3,2)
'Hold the dart like this and _____ _____ at the bull's eye.'

8 The dust that comes from a nuclear explosion. (7)
'The trouble with nuclear _____ is that it is radioactive and highly dangerous.'

10 Solve, deduce. (4,3)
'Don't ask me what the answer is. Try to _____ it _____ for yourself.'

11 Pay attention. (3,2)
'Then I told him what I <u>really</u> thought of him. That made him _____ _____ all right!'

12 Land (of an aeroplane). (5,4)
'Everyone gave a big sigh of relief as soon as they saw the plane _____ _____.'

16 A kind of railway at an amusement park. (10)
'I love the way a _____ railway twists and turns.'

17 Total amount of money taken by a company during the year. (8)
'Did you know that the Little Inkling Company more than doubled its _____ last year?'

18 Become extinguished. (4,3)
'We let the fire _____ itself _____.'

Down

1 Something you no longer need, especially clothing. (4,3)
   'Oxfam is always glad to receive _____-_____ clothing.'

2 Wander. (4,5)
   'The best way to see a town is to park your car and just _____
   _____ for an hour or two.'

4 Make a reservation. (4,2)
   'If you want a ticket for *Hamlet*, you really ought to _____
   _____ now.'

6 Lipstick, face powder, eye shadow, etc. (6)
   'Do you think that men as well as women should use _____?'

7 Improve something by adding or removing small details. (5,2)
   'I haven't got time to repaint the garage door. I think I'll just
   _____ it _____ here and there.'

9 Stay in bed a bit longer in the morning. (3,2)
   'I have to get up at six every day to make the breakfast, so I like
   to _____ _____ on Sunday mornings.'

11 Change from one thing to another. (6,4)
   'We have decided to _____ _____ from oil to gas fired
   central heating.'

13 Discern, just be able to see. (4,3)
   'We could only just _____ _____ the farmhouse in the early
   morning mist.'

14 Ready and waiting to get a place or go into action, etc. (7)
   'On Fridays, all the flights out of Cologne are fully booked, and
   dozens of people are on _____.'

15 Continue. (5,2)
   'After the police arrested the man, the Princess was able to
   _____ _____ with her tour of inspection.'

16 Organise, establish. (3,2)
   'The government has _____ _____ a special committee to
   look into the problem of drug smuggling.'

60 Crazy headlines 4

Underline the spelling mistake in these newspaper headlines.

1 CONTROVERSY OVER SUNDAY OPENING OF INDIAN SHOPS IN CARACAS: SHOPOWNERS SAY THEY INTEND TO <u>CURRY</u> ON AS USUAL

2 YOUNGSTERS LUCK IN AT VILLAGE FEAST

3 OLD PEOPLE ADVISED TO TRAP UP WELL DURING COLD SPELL

4 ANGRY SCENES IN CONGRESS: BRAZIL'S PRESIDENT WASHES OUT AT OPPOSITION'S 'DISHONEST TACTICS'

5 OFFICIALS CRITICISED FOR SCANNING ABOUT IN EXPENSIVE CARS AT TAXPAYERS' EXPENSE

6 WHOLE TRIBES WIRED OUT BY FLU EPIDEMIC

7 SEA BREEZES OVER IN COLDEST WINTER IN LIVING MEMORY

8 VILLAGERS MOUNT CAMPAIGN TO STUMP OUT TREE VANDALISM

9 CAT, TWENTY-FIVE YEARS OLD, PUSSES AWAY AFTER SHORT ILLNESS

10 SPECIAL INVESTIGATOR PROMISES TO ROOF OUT CORRUPTION IN THE HOUSE OF COMMONS

Answers

Test 1

1	was like	9	get back
2	go with	10	take down
3	get in	11	is for
4	took back	12	takes off
5	come from	13	go on
6	come back	14	came off
7	go away	15	get up
8	is about		

Test 2

1	away	9	through
2	back	10	with
3	for	11	up
4	on	12	off
5	from	13	around
6	like	14	into
7	about	15	after (x 2)
8	over		

Test 3

1	back	9	to
2	from	10	on
3	in	11	along
4	before	12	into
5	round	13	up
6	forward	14	off
7	across	15	about
8	out		

Test 4

1	across	6	round
2	away	7	into
3	on	8	behind
4	back	9	down
5	to	10	over

Test 5

1 It should be 'the street lights went off'.
2 It should be 'Gone away'.
3 It should be 'I've really gone off it lately'.
4 It should be 'flu virus going round'.
5 It should be 'Do go on!'
6 It should be 'when he went through his pockets'.
7 It should be 'really goes with'.
8 It should be 'can go without water'.
9 It should be 'enough food to go round'.
10 It should be 'go through' or 'go over' the instructions.

Test 6

1	taken down	6	take off
2	take it back	7	take after
3	take out	8	taken in
4	take up	9	take it up
5	taken over	10	take on

Test 7

1 c
2 e
3 a
4 d
5 b

Test 8

1	False	6	True
2	True	7	True
3	False	8	False
4	False	9	True
5	True	10	True

Test 9

1	get	9	broken
2	take	10	stay
3	threw	11	see
4	put	12	comes
5	chop	13	take
6	lie	14	cuts
7	goes	15	dropped
8	call		

Test 10
1 break	9 trade
2 stay	10 bought
3 give	11 drawing
4 keep	12 gone
5 show	13 dig
6 get	14 deal (x2)
7 calling	15 brought
8 handed	

Test 11
1 get down	9 lie down
2 take down	10 put down
3 turn down	11 write down
4 break down	12 track down
5 cut down	13 wear down
6 come down	14 stand down
7 look down	15 let down
8 put down	

Test 12
1 dried	9 work
2 took	10 helping
3 cuts	11 drop
4 throw	12 slipped
5 rub	13 stand
6 pick	14 wipe
7 fallen	15 pass
8 show	

Test 13
1 stay	6 frighten
2 running	7 slipped
3 take	8 tow
4 look	9 fade
5 break	10 sent

Test 14
Caption a	away
Caption b	down
Caption c	in
Caption d	off
Caption e	out

1 'How nice of you to drop in!'
2 'I'll soon work it out.'
3 'Attendance has been dropping off lately.'
4 'You should have seen the fish that got away!'
5 'He has slowed down a lot since his operation.'

Test 15
1 g	6 i
2 h	7 b
3 c	8 f
4 a	9 j
5 e	10 d

Test 16
1 puts off	a	look into
2 go off	b	hang up
3 hangs up	c	fell through
4 fell out	d	stand for
5 cut down	e	put off
6 stand for	f	make up
7 fell through	g	gone off
8 make up	h	go out
9 look into	i	fallen out
10 go out	j	cut down

1 e	6 d
2 g	7 c
3 b	8 f
4 i	9 a
5 j	10 h

Test 17
1 cut out	a	tuck in
2 give away	b	tore off
3 drop in	c	give away
4 turn in	d	cut out
5 tear off	e	hang up
6 look into	f	turn in
7 break off	g	look into
8 tucks in	h	turn around
9 turn around	i	drop in
10 hang up	j	break off

1 d	6 g
2 c	7 j
3 i	8 a
4 f	9 h
5 b	10 e

Test 18

1. 'The artist has tried to give the idea of "Young Love" but I don't think it quite comes off.'
2. 'It's not likely to take off today, is it?'
3. 'Don't forget to switch off the light before you go to bed.'
4. 'Are they supposed to come off like that?'
5. 'He never takes his hat off in public.'
6. 'When he is bored, he simply switches off.'

Test 19

1	fall through	a	look up
2	dry up	b	make up
3	puts off	c	catch on
4	make up	d	dry up
5	look up	e	run across
6	see through	f	see through
7	fall off	g	fall through
8	take back	h	take back
9	run across	i	fall off
10	catch on	j	put off

1	g	6	f
2	d	7	i
3	j	8	h
4	b	9	e
5	a	10	c

Test 20

1. He goes out at the same time every night.
2. 'Please put all the bones back in their proper place.'
3. 'That's the end of summer. Time to put the clocks back.'
4. 'But WHY do you want to blow up the Houses of Parliament?'
5. 'Come on, blow up the balloon and let's get started.'
6. 'Now don't let the fire go out!'

Test 21

1	let off	a	set off
2	stand by	b	leaked out
3	look over	c	look over
4	clear up	d	let off
5	cut down	e	clear up
6	cover up	f	playing at
7	bump into	g	bumped into
8	set off	h	cut down
9	playing at	i	stand by
10	leaks out	j	cover up

1	d	6	j
2	i	7	g
3	c	8	a
4	e	9	f
5	h	10	b

Test 22

1	outfit	6	outburst
2	outlook	7	outcry
3	outbreak	8	outcast
4	outlet	9	outcome
5	outlay	10	outset

Test 23

1. If you don't feel like cooking, go and get something from the Mexican takeaway.
2. The joys of modern travel: a five-mile tailback on the freeway!
3. A non-stick frying pan! The scientific breakthrough we've all been waiting for!
4. It takes minutes to fill your basket, and hours to get through the supermarket checkout.
5. A bank holdup.
6. If the traffic gets too bad, pull into a lay-by and have a rest.

Test 24

1	handout	6	breakdown
2	mixed-up	7	fallout
3	holdup	8	outfit
4	outlook	9	take-off
5	make-up	10	standby

Test 25

1	c	6	b
2	a	7	d
3	d	8	b
4	b	9	a
5	a	10	c

Test 26

1 You can stay in your car: this is a drive-in movie.
2 These shoes have no laces: they are slip-on shoes.
3 This is not an aerosol deodorant: it is a roll-on deodorant.
4 The crooks used this as a getaway vehicle.
5 This is a pop-up book.
6 This is a pick-up truck.
7 This is cast-off clothing.
8 There is a sale on: everything at knockdown prices.
9 The shop owner does not live here: it is a lock-up shop.
10 This shed is not freestanding: it is a lean-to shed.

Test 27

1	built-up	6	stuck-up
2	throwaway	7	follow-up
3	run-down	8	see-through
4	mixed-up	9	takeover
5	worn-out	10	stand-offish

Test 28

1	a lean-to	5	make-up
2	a pinup	6	a hangover
3	a pick-up	7	a lie in
4	a handout	8	a showdown

Test 29

1	d	6	b
2	f	7	j
3	a	8	g
4	i	9	c
5	h	10	e

i	7	vi	10
ii	4	vii	1
iii	3	viii	5
iv	9	ix	2
v	6	x	8

Test 30

1 'OK, everybody. Tea break over. Time to get back to work!'
2 'We speak out against injustice wherever we find it.'
3 'The problem is that we've run out of matches.'
4 'My wife has walked out on me. I can't think why.'
5 'Please don't wait up for me.'
6 'This is what happens when you fall behind with the rent.'

Test 31

1 come up against
2 get down to
3 run out of
4 cut down on
5 look up to
6 give in to
7 put up with
8 listen in on
9 catch up with
10 look forward to

Test 32

1 'SEND AWAY FOR YOUR COPY TODAY! ONLY TWENTY-FIVE DOLLARS!'
2 'What it really boils down to, then, is that you don't love me any more. Is that it?'
3 'You'll never get away with it!'
4 Not everyone looks forward to Christmas.
5 'Don't worry, he's just a puppy. He'll soon grow out of it.'
6 'It's no good going on about it – you lost, and that's all there is to it.'

Test 33

1	i	6	b
2	d	7	h
3	a	8	f
4	j	9	e
5	g	10	c

i	7	vi	10
ii	4	vii	1
iii	3	viii	5
iv	9	ix	2
v	6	x	8

Test 34

1	c	6	g
2	f	7	e
3	j	8	h
4	b	9	a
5	i	10	d

i	4	vi	1
ii	8	vii	6
iii	2	viii	5
iv	10	ix	7
v	9	x	3

Test 35

1	blow up	11	let on
2	brush up	12	make up
3	call for	13	own up
4	carry on	14	pull out
5	come in	15	put off
6	come up	16	rip off
7	cut out	17	settle down
8	fill in	18	turn up
9	fit in	19	wear out
10	go on	20	work out

```
S E T T L E D O W N J L
E T U O L L U P O I K E
C A R R Y O N A R L S T
L L N F B S P N K L X T
B R U S H U P D O I R O
L U P S E Y M U U E I N
O L E K S P F F T U P C
W E A R O U T B F O O A
U M I G A E N I I S F L
P U N W O M M F T O F L
O R M E C O M E I N T O
T U O T U C N B N Y E R
```

Test 36

1	go on	6	clear up
2	think over	7	stand for
3	come round	8	pull out
4	come into	9	brush up
5	look into	10	make up

Test 37

1	give away	6	draw up
2	step up	7	made up
3	carry out	8	fill in
4	break off	9	put forward
5	clear up	10	turn down

Test 38

1	show up	6	touch on
2	run down	7	tip off
3	fall out	8	come round
4	split up	9	fall off
5	think over	10	throw away

Test 39

1	settle down	6	pick out
2	brush up	7	do without
3	strip off	8	explain away
4	go round	9	let on
5	stand for	10	come into

Test 40

1	cut down	6	slip up
2	set off	7	work out
3	blow up	8	carry on
4	call for	9	shake off
5	wear out	10	fit in

Test 41

1	dropped in	6	given up
2	turns up	7	looked through
3	play down	8	pull away
4	pull out of	9	get away
5	put off		

Test 42

1 DR MARTEN'S BOYS TOLD: 'FACE UP TO YOUR RESPONSIBILITIES'
2 MAN ADMITS TO KNIFE ATTACK ON NOISY NEIGHBOURS: 'IT WAS IMPOSSIBLE TO PUT UP WITH THEM ANY MORE,' HE SAYS.
3 PEOPLE IN BIG CARS ALWAYS TRY TO CATCH UP WITH THE CAR IN FRONT
4 SCUBA DIVER 'DROPPED IN' ON SUBMARINE. 'I JUST WANTED TO SAY HELLO.'
5 OVERPRICED HAIRDRESSERS COME IN FOR A LOT OF CRITICISM
6 OUTBREAK OF MYSTERY ILLNESS AMONGST POULTRY. MINISTRY OF AGRICULTURE PROMISES TO CHECK UP ON IT.
7 HOW TO STAY CALM: CUT DOWN ON THE AMOUNT OF COFFEE YOU DRINK!

8 ECONOMISTS PREDICT BIG INCREASE IN POTATO SALES. FARMERS ADVISED TO <u>CASH</u> IN ON THIS OPPORTUNITY

9 STOP COMPARING YOURSELF WITH YOUR NEIGHBOUR, ADVISES SOCIAL WORKER: 'USELESS TO TRY TO <u>KEEP</u> UP WITH THE JONESES'

10 POST OFFICE PROMISES BETTER MAIL DELIVERY: 'HAPPY TO <u>FALL</u> IN WITH CUSTOMERS' WISHES'

Test 43
1 bring up
2 make out
3 shouting at
4 mixing up
5 dawned on
6 getting at
7 crop up
8 wiped out
9 run down
10 plumped for

Test 44
1 fooling around
2 pouring down
3 pulls through
4 make out
5 doubled up
6 cropping up
7 simmer down
8 step up
9 shouting at
10 stuck by

Test 45
1 run
2 shrug
3 Roll
4 freshen
5 mixing
6 live
7 seize
8 hush
9 dawned
10 turn

Test 46
1 skate over
2 blends in
3 wiped out
4 run away
5 size up
6 copes with
7 brought up
8 rinse out
9 leaked out
10 sound out

Test 47
1 go, hang, knock
2 lash, strike, hit
3 fork, shell, pay
4 end, land, finish
5 drop, look, call

a hold
b butt
c rushed
d playing
e stock

Test 48
1 drag on
2 meddle with
3 getting at
4 rub in
5 snapped up
6 flaked out
7 jumped at
8 wade through
9 rambled on
10 plumped for

Test 49
1 bite off
2 throw out
3 turn over
4 put off
5 look after (x 2)
6 comes out
7 runs away
8 pick up

A Don't bite off more than you can chew.

B The sun always comes out after the rain.

C Look after the pennies and the pounds will look after themselves.

D See a pin and pick it up, and all day long you'll have good luck.

E Never put off till tomorrow what you can do today.

F He who fights and runs away, Lives to fight another day.

G Don't throw out the baby with the bath water.

H Turn over a new leaf.

Test 50
1 a
2 c
3 b
4 d
5 a
6 b
7 c
8 a
9 d
10 b

Test 51
1 b
2 c
3 d
4 c
5 c
6 c
7 b
8 a
9 a
10 a

Test 52
1 a
2 d
3 c
4 c
5 b
6 a
7 d
8 b
9 b
10 c

Test 53

1	b	6	b
2	d	7	d
3	b	8	c
4	c	9	a
5	d	10	c

Test 54

1	d	6	b
2	b	7	c
3	a	8	d
4	c	9	c
5	a	10	b

Test 55

1	b	6	d
2	a	7	b
3	c	8	a
4	d	9	d
5	b	10	c

Test 56

1 MEAT PRICES ARE DOWN AGAIN. HOUSEWIVES ADVISED TO SHOP AROUND FOR THE BEST BARGAINS
2 DON'T KNOCK OFF EARLY ON FRIDAY AFTERNOONS, WORKERS WARNED
3 LOCAL COUNCIL TELL GRAFFITI ARTISTS TO 'BUZZ OFF'
4 NEW WEBSITE BOASTS BIGGEST ENCYCLOPAEDIA OF THE WORLD'S WINES. 'WELL WORTH DIPPING INTO,' SAY THE EXPERTS
5 SAILING IS NOW THIRD MOST POPULAR HOBBY. 'MEN LOVE TO MESS ABOUT IN BOATS,' SAYS LEISURE FIRM.
6 SWIMMER'S DEATH SPARKS OFF A SAFETY ENQUIRY
7 AMAZON EXPLORERS DECIDE TO PRESS ON DESPITE THE HEAT
8 'ATTENDANCE AT WATER POLO EVENTS DROPPING OFF' SAYS OFFICIAL REPORT.
9 IMMIGRANT WORKERS FEEL ALIENATED: HAVE A HARD TIME FITTING IN
10 EIGHTY-YEAR-OLD JUDGE CRITICISED FOR NODDING OFF DURING TRIAL. 'IF HE CAN'T STAY AWAKE, HE SHOULD RETIRE,' LAWYER COMMENTS

Test 57

1 FIRE BRIGADE ON ALERT AS VANDALS THREATEN TO BURN DOWN FARM BUILDINGS
2 BRITISH ATHLETE INTENDS TO TRY FOR NEW WORLD RECORD AT COMING COMMONWEALTH GAMES
3 NEW ZEALAND NOCTURNAL GROUND PARROT IN DANGER: 'WE MUST CONSERVE ITS HABITAT OR IT WILL DIE OUT SOON,' SAYS LEADING NATURALIST.
4 SHOCK MEDICAL REPORT: STUDENTS CRACKING UP UNDER EXAMINATION PRESSURE
5 POLICE SURROUND PRISON AS DANGEROUS CRIMINALS TRY TO BREAK OUT
6 SECURITY TIGHTENED UP AT AIRPORTS AS NEW TERRORIST CAMPAIGN BEGINS
7 AFTER FIFTEEN YEARS, HUSBAND FINALLY TUMBLES TO WIFE'S LOVER
8 MANCHESTER MAN BUMPS INTO LONG-LOST BROTHER IN NEW YORK NIGHTCLUB
9 LADY CHATTERLEY TO MARRY HER GARDENER: 'I JUST HOPE IT WORKS OUT FOR THEM,' SAY HER PARENTS
10 HOUSEWIVES TIRED OF BEING TIED TO THE KITCHEN SINK: 'THERE MUST BE MORE TO LIFE THAN WASHING UP,' THEY SAY

Test 58

Across

1 come down
4 send off
7 outbreak
8 do
10 bowl over
13 down
14 on
15 string

Down

1 cast off
2 end
3 offset
5 note down
6 skate
9 own
10 book
11 out
12 run
16 in

Test 59

Across

3 look out
5 aim at
8 fallout
10 work out
11 sit up
12 touch down
16 switchback
17 turnover
18 burn out

Down

1 cast-off
2 walk about
4 book up
6 make-up
7 touch up
9 lie in
11 switch over
13 make out
14 standby
15 carry on
16 set up

Test 60

1 CONTROVERSY OVER SUNDAY OPENING OF INDIAN SHOPS IN CARACAS: SHOPOWNERS SAY THEY INTEND TO <u>CARRY</u> ON AS USUAL

2 YOUNGSTERS <u>TUCK</u> IN AT VILLAGE FEAST

3 OLD PEOPLE ADVISED TO <u>WRAP</u> UP WELL DURING COLD SPELL

4 ANGRY SCENES IN CONGRESS: BRAZIL'S PRESIDENT <u>LASHES</u> OUT AT OPPOSITION'S 'DISHONEST TACTICS'

5 OFFICIALS CRITICISED FOR <u>SWANNING</u> ABOUT IN EXPENSIVE CARS AT TAXPAYERS' EXPENSE

6 WHOLE TRIBES <u>WIPED</u> OUT BY FLU EPIDEMIC

7 SEA <u>FREEZES</u> OVER IN COLDEST WINTER IN LIVING MEMORY

8 VILLAGERS MOUNT CAMPAIGN TO <u>STAMP</u> OUT TREE VANDALISM

9 CAT, TWENTY-FIVE YEARS OLD, <u>PASSES</u> AWAY AFTER SHORT ILLNESS

10 SPECIAL INVESTIGATOR PROMISES TO <u>ROOT</u> OUT CORRUPTION IN THE HOUSE OF COMMONS

Test Your way to success in English
Test Your Vocabulary

0582 45166 3

0582 45167 1

0582 45168 X

0582 45169 8

0582 45170 1